Time for
TheTalk

Time for
TheTalk

LEADING YOUR SON INTO TRUE MANHOOD

STEVE ZOLLOS

Time For The Talk
© 2011 by Stephen Zollos

Trade Paperback ISBN: 978-1-936908-17-2

eBook ISBN
Mobi format: ISBN 978-1-936908-18-9
epub format: ISBN 978-1-936908-19-6

Published by Shepherd Press
P.O. Box 24
Wapwallopen, Pennsylvania 18660

Page design and typesetting by Lakeside Design Plus
Cover design by Tobias' Outerwear for Books

First Printing, 2011
Printed in the United States of America

VP   22 21 20 19 18 17 16 15 14 13 12 11
14 13 12 11 10 9   8   7   6   5   4   3   2   1

Library of Congress Cataloging-in-Publication Data
Zollos, Stephen.
    Time for the talk : leading your son into true manhood / Steve Zollos.
        p. cm.
    Includes bibliographical references and index.
    ISBN 978-1-936908-17-2 (trade pbk. : alk. paper)—ISBN 978-1-936908-18-9 (mobi ebook edition)—ISBN 978-1-936908-19-6 (epub ebook edition)
        1. Sex instruction for boys. 2. Sex instruction for boys—Religious aspects. 3. Sexual ethics. 4. Fathers and sons. I. Title.
    HQ41.Z65 2011
    649'.65088241—dc23
                                                        2011025879

eBook Coupons
Free eBook for the purchaser of *Time For the Talk* in Trade Paperback format
Go to: http://www.shepherdpress.com/ebooks
Mobi file for Kindle: TALKM01
ePub file for iPad: TALKE01

To my sons: Stepheno, Phillip, Emerson, and Andreas

May your love abound more and more in knowledge and depth of insight, so that you may be able to discern what is best and may be pure and blameless until the day of Christ, filled with the fruit of righteousness that comes through Jesus Christ—to the glory and praise of God.

—Philippians 1:9-11

Contents

Foreword

In daily conversation, "The Talk" is usually polite shorthand for "telling children where babies come from." Here, however, I give the phrase a big promotion and a much more significant job description. Let me explain.

This book is written to you, the father of a young son. It is built on the conviction that raising your son is really no big deal ... unless you plan on him becoming humble, courageous, morally pure, faithful, selfless, and self-controlled: in other words, a godly young man. To get there your son will need a lot of help, and you, as his father, are certainly the best man for the job.

Through "The Talk," as I define it in this book, you will help your son learn to trust in the Lord, and not his own understanding. You will open a channel of communication based on truth and love that will endure for life. You will talk directly to him—and with him—about difficult subjects you two have probably never ventured to discuss before. If done in the encouraging way I suggest, you will become a trusted confidant—his lifelong friend.

If this doesn't sound easy, you're right. In fact, if you haven't tried it, it's probably harder than you think. That's why I wrote this book. Within these pages I have made every attempt to integrate the truth of Scripture into the process and the topics associated with "The Talk." Having "The Talk" with your son will require prayer, patience, and your own willingness to change. Think about that for a moment. Unless you are a very rare breed of father, this book is going to suggest that you need to alter certain ways of thinking and living. To serve your son the way you need to, to help him become the man God wants him to be, you are going to have to change. That's what you're signing up for here. Your son is getting older every day and, as I suggest throughout this book, it's best if you can begin The Talk when he is about ten or eleven, or as soon thereafter as possible. Are you ready to help him? Are you ready to change?

This book is based largely on experience I have gained in raising my own four boys as well as my twenty years of health care experience, much of which has been working in the community. The techniques and perspectives I share are not sure-fire solutions, but I have made every effort to make sure that they line up with the gospel of grace and the relevant teachings from Scripture. To the extent that they do line up, this book offers wisdom from God—the best possible guidance you can give your son in this broken, fallen world.

One day your son will walk his own path. He will do some things right and some things wrong, because in this life we will never be perfect or sinless. He's a lot like you that way, but through The Talk you will help him avoid many mistakes that otherwise he would almost certainly make—mistakes that can be harmful, corrupting, even disastrous. You will also be positioning yourself to be there for him when he does stumble. Because of you and how you handled The Talk, he will never have to say, "I just didn't know," or "I didn't have anyone to turn to for advice."

Using this material and building a foundation of open, honest communication that it can establish, your son can gain knowledge, wisdom, and maturity beyond his years. You will be giving him what he needs to steer through the moral and spiritual confusion of this world and make wise, godly, character-forming decisions. In the process, you will be making a friend for life.

Steve Zollos

A Preface to Mothers

Before we get started, I want to address mothers.

Ladies, everything you find in this book can be used to excellent advantage in households where a father is absent, unable, or unwilling to assume his proper role in this area. While the language of this book addresses fathers, you who may be in the role of both mother and father can take heart. There are two ways you can use this material to serve your son.

First, you can apply everything in this book by having The Talk with your son yourself. If you choose this approach, I strongly encourage you not to skip or skim over any topic appropriate to the age of your son.

As an alternative, I know households in which a trusted male leader has effectively walked boys through The Talk, either all of it or just selected portions. If you choose this route, both you and the man (perhaps a member of your immediate family, local church, or a close family friend) should become familiar with this material. Discuss what areas you would prefer to cover with your son yourself. As for the remaining areas indicate which, if any, you would like to have emphasized. As the boy's mother,

11

you should know everything your son is being taught. You and the trusted friend need to be clear on the goals of The Talk and the boundaries of the conversation. The trusted friend may be the one actually presenting some or all of The Talk, but it must be done under your temporary, delegated authority as the boy's parent. The responsibility that it be done, and done well, still resides with you.

Regardless of your situation, you can rest in the assurance that God cares deeply that your son be well served in this area. As you read this book and apply its teachings in ways that fit your circumstances, God will provide the grace you need to serve your son effectively.

> My son, do not forget my teaching, but keep my commands in your heart, for they will prolong your life many years and bring you prosperity. Let love and faithfulness never leave you; bind them around your neck, write them on the tablet of your heart. Then you will win favor and a good name in the sight of God and man.
>
> —Proverbs 3:1–4 NIV

Preparations

CHAPTER 1

Much More Than a Talk

C hances are you're just like me in some regards. I love my children and I want to see them succeed, and I'm sure you want the same for your children. That's why you picked up this book. Raising my boys has been the most fun, adventurous, and sometimes the most nerve-wracking joy of my life. Boys are always full of surprises—some pleasant, and some, well, some that are not so pleasant. But I love my boys—bruises, mistakes, apathy, pride and all—there is no doubt about that. One day I came home from work to find my boys playing with, of all things, bees!

Of Boys and Bumble Bees

It had been a long hard day at the office, finally I pulled into the driveway. "Home at last," I thought out loud with a long exhausted sigh. No sooner had the words left my mouth than my son, then eight years old, came running from the back yard and through the garage to greet me.

"Dad, Dad, Dad," he said excitedly helping to open my door. "Dad, you've got to come into the back yard and see what we're doing!" He was excited and as out of breath as an eight-year-old gets.

"Okay, okay," I replied, feigning excitement. "I'll be out, but first I need to say hello to your mom and change my clothes." It was really my escape route, I should have known it wouldn't work, but it was the best I could come up with on the spur of the moment.

"No, Dad, you gotta come now, you have to see what we're doing. We're nailing bees!" he said wide-eyed with a broad smile that beamed with excitement. His pride in their activity was in full bloom. "Nailing bees?" I said with trepidation, repeating his words, "I guess you're right, I do need to see what you're doing."

Stepheno scurried through the garage and into the back yard. I followed him through the back door and there were my sons, Stepheno and Phillip, with yellow plastic baseball bats in hand. I watched the young "Mickey Mantle" and "Babe Ruth" smiling broadly as they stared at the split-rail fence with wild anticipation.

Then, only a moment later, a large black and yellow carpenter bee came hovering down to find his nest that was located in the gate, and the boys started swinging for the fences!

Whoosh! Phillip swung just over the bee. Whoosh! Stepheno swung, barely missing Phillip, who was winding up for yet another stroke. Instinctively I stepped out of harm's way and as I did so I heard a hollow "wap" and witnessed the hapless bee smack against the wall and fall to the ground. I wasn't sure if it was stunned or dead.

So that's what "nailing bees" is all about, I thought and I was just about to launch into a controlled tirade that would effectively explain the dangers of nailing bees and put this foolishness to an end when Stepheno stopped me before I could get two words out of my mouth.

16

"No, Dad, watch!" he said, and I watched in disbelief as he proceeded to pick up the bee by a wing.

"What in the world now?" I asked myself incredulously. My boys, still carrying the bee, marched militarily into the middle of the yard where my grass was noticeably torn up and a mound of clay about eighteen inches high had been skillfully constructed.

Kneeling down my son reached behind him and pulled out a small nail and a hammer that he had commandeered from my workbench. Then he proceeded to literally nail the bee to the mound of dirt!

It was then that the picture came fully into focus. This was a home school science project gone awry! Here in the middle of the yard they had created a specimen board and were pinning bugs to it to put them on display. But these weren't ordinary bugs; this was a nest of big black and yellow bees! There must have been twenty-five of them nailed to that mound of dirt.

On the one hand, I thought, "not bad for six and eight-year-old boys." I mean, it took some guts and it was creative too—but way too dangerous. They could have been stung, and based on the number of bees on that mound they could have really been stung repeatedly. I could tell by their proud smiles that they felt they were doing me a great service. After all, they knew that I would have had to spray those bees anyway since they were nesting right in the gate.

I was just about to give them a good talking to about the dangers of "nailing bees" when my wife came out the back door and onto the deck.

"Did you see what these boys have been doing?" I asked, fully anticipating a look of horror and an apology for her lack of oversight. I thought that I might have to keep her from launching into a tirade about the dangers of "nailing bees" herself, but to my surprise she answered in a calm, almost angelic voice.

"Yes I have," she began. "In fact, they haven't come inside all day. They haven't once asked me 'what's to eat?' or 'what's there to do?' Why, I've gotten more done in the house today than I have in the last three weeks!"

"Well, isn't that just fine," I thought. "I guess I'll have to do all the scolding myself." The only question was who I scold first, the boys or my wife.

I took a deep breath and turned to my wife. She was beautiful, disarming, totally calm, and smiling radiantly—even glowing. I turned to my sons. They were still smiling broadly, excited and fully anticipating a "well done" from their dad. I looked back at my wife and then at my boys again. It was then that I had an epiphany.

The bees-nest was all but eradicated already, so my kids were no longer in any real danger. My wife appeared especially beautiful, energetic, and happy. I could discuss the "science project" later, and why not?

"Well," I finally said, "you boys be careful when you nail those bees, and use a pair of pliers to pick them up." Then I marched through the back door and into the house with my lovely wife and enjoyed the first peaceful meal for two that we had had in a long time.

The Moral of the Story: Perspective Matters.

To my boys "nailing bees" was a wild and fun-filled science experiment, not to mention an important service to their Dad. To Mom, "nailing bees" meant a heavenly and productive afternoon. To me, "nailing bees" went from being just plain crazy to being somewhat creative, and then, when my calmer self prevailed, I finally realized that "nailing bees" that day was a gift to us all. As it turned out, "nailing bees" was one of our most memorable family moments. Perspective matters.

And so it is with The Talk. Sure, there have been difficult things to walk through as a parent. Sure, your boys haven't made all the right decisions and I'm sure it has cost you time, tears, and no small amount of money somewhere along the way. In spite of all that, being a dad is a wonderful adventure that brings life at its fullest right to your doorstep.

Now that your son is getting older, The Talk should be seen as another excellent opportunity and not a dreaded task. You can make it enjoyable, even a great memory, and the fulfillment of a critical responsibility that every boy's father should undertake.

With the right perspective having The Talk with your son not only becomes easier, but fun. As you teach your son about life you will have the opportunity to teach him about Jesus. We were created to be virtuous. We were created to love and obey God, but we have, each one of us, chosen our own way—apart from God.

It follows then that teaching your son to be a "true" or virtuous man is really teaching him about the wide and narrow gates. You will be showing him how to stay off the broad road in order to avoid death and destruction. More importantly, you will be teaching him how to know and stay on the narrow road and in so doing step into the joy that the Lord has set before him.

I don't know about you, but for me just the thought of leading my son into true manhood, showing him the way to life and encouraging him in his walk with the Lord, fills me with excitement. It is one of the most important things I will ever do.

Much More Than a Talk

As your boy has grown, your job as a father has become more complex and challenging. You have gone from meeting essential needs (such as changing diapers), to training ("Don't play in the street."), to teaching (assisting with school lessons and helping your son discern right from wrong). Once you recognize your boy is coming of age and is ready for The Talk (readiness is discussed in chapter 5), you can begin to undertake your most important task as a father—leading him to submit his life to Christ.

Leading your son into true manhood is a great honor and a serious responsibility. It's a process that takes many years and can be profoundly rewarding. It is, in fact, the ultimate goal of raising a boy.

So much of your leadership to this point has been preparation for this crucial step. By discussing the topics presented in "Time for The Talk," you will be making your son aware of the truth concerning many things that were previously hidden from him.

You will be equipping him to enter true manhood, a passage that many young men today simply never make. You will be opening a new door of communication and trust between you and your son.

When it comes to raising your son, every day is important, but not every day is equal. There are particular days, moments, and seasons that are absolutely crucial. If you miss these windows of opportunity, it will hinder some of your other efforts. If, on the other hand, you are able to take advantage of these opportune moments, you can lock in the gains and even make up for many past failures.

This book is about one of those especially important seasons—probably the single most crucial season in the process of leading your son into true manhood. This book is about The Talk.

I have seen this process at work in my relationship with all four of my sons, currently ages twelve to twenty-one. As I have sought to lead them each into manhood, all I have learned about The Talk has been backed up by my research, my study of Scripture, and my conversations and interactions with many other fathers.

It is essential that you be the one to help your son understand the changes his body is going through, and the many joys and perils he will face as a man. You will be telling him the truth about things he has seen and heard but thought he could never ask about, and introducing him to some things that he has probably never even imagined. To do this effectively you will need to contrast the biblical view of sexuality with the world's view. No doubt he has learned much from the world that is ungodly in its basis.

How to Use This Book

The Talk should be a series of personal conversations with your son, and this book has been written to help you make those conversations most profitable. In that light, it is important from the outset that you understand how this book can best be used. Here is a simple ten-step process for you to follow:

1. Read this book from cover to cover, becoming familiar with all the material.

2. Prepare to have The Talk with your son.

Use the topical outline found in the back of this book as you talk with your son.

3. As you cover each topic, check them off on the outline itself; in that way you will have a reminder of what has been covered and what might need to be covered at another time. This is especially important if you are starting to have conversations when your son is twelve years old or younger.

4. Bring this book with you when you are using it simply as a reference tool. Having read it all the way through you probably won't need it, but it's nice to have it handy just in case.

5. If you are having a follow-up discussion, don't be afraid to cover important material a second time.

6. Tell your story, your way, treating your son like a young man. He will appreciate and remember this time in his life, and he will value the things you share with him.

7. Keep it positive. A good rule of thumb is to discuss five blessings associated with honoring God in our actions for every consequence you discuss that is associated with disobeying God. Our goal is that our sons choose to trust God as they recognize his love and mercy for them. While there is a place for having a healthy "fear of the Lord," The Talk should major on God's love, grace, and kindness.

8. Keep the gospel at the center of your discussion. Manhood is all about knowing and being known by God.

9. Consider a short time of prayer with your son as you approach each major area of discussion. Ask, seek, and knock for wisdom, and don't forget to give God the glory for topics already covered, and the truth that is going forth in your relationship with your son.

10. Have fun. Don't be surprised when your son doesn't receive everything you tell him—or anything at all for that matter. Simply be faithful and trust God when things don't seem to be going well.

With these things in mind, you're ready to begin your journey of leading your son into manhood.

The World Has Changed

Growing up has never been easy, not for boys. For many of you fathers reading this book, fistfights, police chases, and broken hearts seemed to be waiting around every corner during your teen years—but the world we see today isn't the world you grew up in. Not even close. Back then there was at least some protection from the dirt of the world. Today, a boy steps off the school bus and into a place you and I never conceived of in our youth. Gangs, drugs, shootings, condoms, sex, pornography, and perversion are everywhere. Worst of all, it's largely accepted, tolerated, or condoned by those in authority.

Oh, so your son is in private school? Or he's home-schooled? Do you really think that makes things different for him? Maybe a little bit, but don't let that give you a false sense of security. That young man still lives in a world hugely more seductive and radically more damaging than the one you knew at his age. Have you listened to his music lately? Have you taken a walk around your neighborhood? Do you have any idea what a typical group of young people talks about in private? Have you heard the language, seen the actions, and understood the values being promoted on movie, television, videogame, computer, and cell phone screens? In the time that you've been on the internet, have you seen things that you would never want your son to see, even accidentally? How much more time does he spend online than you?

You and I would be seriously thrown off balance if we were transported back to being a sixteen-year-old in today's teen environment. Life has become a lot harder, especially for adolescent boys. If your son is going to stand a chance in this fast-paced, micro-chipped, image-laden, values-barren landscape, you had better be there for him.

Thankfully these changes in the world are not new to God. You can encourage your son with the powerful reality that Jesus faced every temptation that he will ever face. He successfully endured each temptation so that he could help you and your son withstand this "modern" attack on purity.

It's your son's life that's on the line, but it's your responsibility. It's your God-given calling to lead him and teach him to become a leader himself, to the glory of God.

"The Talk" Is More than a Talk

Society calls it "The Talk," but the phrase is often used almost as a joke, a virtual admission of failure. No young man has ever been helped by some brief, awkward, and hopelessly vague lecture about birds, bees, and girls. How have we come to the point that such an important subject is typically handled so poorly, even among Christians?

As fathers, we are tempted to abdicate our responsibility in this area. We get lazy and take the easy way out: we lie to ourselves. We think, *My boy knows about these things. He's not ignorant. He's a good kid. He'll do fine.* As a result, we deliver a useless little talk or skip it completely.

The truth is that your son doesn't know as he ought to know, and in this area he is ignorant. He was born ignorant, and nothing in society can properly fix that. No random bits of misinformation about sex; no value-neutral program of sex education; no myths or urban legends; no sensual movies or glimpses of pornography; not even actual sexual contact can ever truly teach a boy about what it means to be a man.

Yes, many boys do understand a few things about sexuality and manhood—in a vague, hazy sort of way, but that's not nearly good enough. In fact, incomplete or inaccurate information can be far more harmful than no information at all! It's true that a boy can navigate through the changes and perils of growing up without the advantage of a father's godly leadership. It happens all the time, but it's a poor Plan B. Just look at all the lost young men in today's world who had to try to find their own way. Now imagine if their fathers had really walked beside them with loving wisdom during their teen years. Many of them would certainly be very different men today.

Until you have had The Talk with your son, in the way it ought to be done, most of what he thinks he knows about becoming a man will have been picked up from friends, movies, television, the internet, his own feelings, or unhelpful books and magazines. These are hardly reliable sources. There is only one place your son can learn, not merely accurate information, but the right emphasis, tone, sense of responsibility, and biblical perspective he must have in order to become a true man: He must learn it from you.

Do you feel ill prepared to do that? Maybe you're not sure how to communicate what you need to. Maybe you're not even completely clear about the facts yourself! That's fine. In fact, that's a good place to be. Humility and a sense of your own neediness are much better than foolish self-confidence. Wherever you are on that spectrum of knowledge and confidence, I believe this book can help.

Of course, to be clear about it, when I refer to The Talk or "having The Talk" in this book, I don't necessarily mean just one conversation. There certainly is an important initial conversation a father needs to have with his son. That conversation is the core element of The Talk, and the main focus of this book. What you need to understand from the outset is that both The Talk and this book are about much more than one conversation. They are about getting to a completely new level of father-son communication.

When a dad learns to communicate wisely and effectively with his son, in a way that no other man on earth can come close to matching, The Talk will naturally grow from a single discussion to a lifelong friendship filled with fruitful conversations. Some of these conversations will be planned, and some will be spontaneous, but the amazing secondary benefit of The Talk is that it can open a new door of communication between father and son that changes their relationship forever.

If you have a younger son, even a toddler, consider it a blessing that you are reading this book now. You will have some extra time to prepare both him and yourself for The Talk.

This Book Is for You

This book is for the father who wants to enjoy that strong, open, and honest communication with his son. It provides a complete framework for discussing the key areas of manhood that every boy should learn and understand from his father. You will be provided with a solid basic understanding of how a boy becomes a man. It will build your knowledge of the diverse topics you will need to address as a father giving The Talk. It will also offer you a step-by-step process for having The Talk with your son in the right way.

Using this book as your guide will make it much easier for you to lead that initial conversation. Then, knowing what your son has and has not been taught at any given point in time, you will be able to extend and maintain the conversation throughout your son's adolescence as you continue to encourage him in his ongoing maturation.

Part 1 outlines the importance of your role, presents the biblical definition of manhood, and walks you through the process of preparing to initiate The Talk with your son. Once you have a clear vision of your role and a firm understanding of biblical manhood, you will be ready to begin. Part 2 provides you with all the information you need to lead your son successfully through The Talk itself. Part 3 offers topics for further discussion as your son grows toward adulthood.

So at first, just read through this book, marking it up and making any notes that will be helpful. Then, during The Talk itself, you can use this book as a guide. This material will allow you to lead key conversations effectively, without overloading your son with medical terminology or launching into a theological dissertation. By teaching you how to lead your son through The Talk, this book can help you effect a crucial, positive, and permanent change in your son's life.

From Boy to Man, and from Father to Friend

The unique relationship between father and son is never more sure, pronounced, or satisfying than when a father takes the initiative to lead his boy into manhood. In fact, I believe that many father/son relationships deteriorate as a boy matures because the father never recognizes his need to shift relational gears and continues to treat his now young man like he's still a child.

You may already be aware of how clear and encouraging Scripture is about the necessity and the effectiveness of a father's active involvement in the moral development of his son, but if there was ever a time to be reminded of these passages, it's in this season of your son's life. Without a doubt, there is no one on earth more important than you, his father, in helping your son grow and mature.

A wise son heeds his father's instruction (Proverbs 13:1 NIV).

Listen, my sons, to a father's instruction; pay attention and gain understanding. I give you sound learning, so do not forsake my teaching (Proverbs 4:1-2 NIV).

My son, keep your father's commands and do not forsake your mother's teaching. Bind them upon your heart forever; fasten them around your neck. When you walk, they will guide you; when you sleep, they will watch over you; when you awake, they will speak to you. For these commands are a lamp, this teaching is a light, and the corrections of discipline are the way to life (Proverbs 6:20–23 NIV).

Train a child in the way he should go, and when he is old he will not turn from it (Proverbs 22:6 NIV).

These commandments that I give you today are to be upon your hearts. Impress them on your children. Talk about them when you sit at home and when you walk along the road, when you lie down and when you get up (Deuteronomy 6:5–7 NIV).

The apostle Paul points out some key differences between childhood and manhood. He says it involves how you talk and think and reason.

When I was a child, I talked like a child, I thought like a child, I reasoned like a child. When I became a man, I put childish ways behind me (1 Corinthians 13:11 NIV).

Your boy is becoming a man. He is growing in personal maturity. As a result, the two of you should be starting to talk, think, and reason together differently than before. The relationship itself is growing in maturity. Through The Talk, your son will be encouraged to walk closely with the Lord and at this moment your relationship with him should start to mature as well. Eventually it will become stronger, richer, and deeper—and it will probably stay that way for the rest of your life.

You are becoming a reliable source of honest information, wisdom, and experience for your son. You are becoming a trusted confidant and a lifelong friend.

CHAPTER 1 REVIEW

1. If you hope to build a strong and lasting relationship with your son, you will have to change. It is time to begin the transition from the "command-and-order" mode to one of "friend-and-counselor."
2. The Talk should be seen as more than a single conversation. The over-arching goal of The Talk is that it opens a door to a deep and trusted father-son relationship that lasts a lifetime.
3. God has uniquely gifted you to lead your son into true manhood.
4. Look for, and expect, your relationship with your son to begin maturing. Consider how you need to change to

promote a strong, lasting relationship with your young man as he continues to mature.

5. Pray with your son as you begin each topic. Rely on the Lord for the wisdom you need to lead your son into true manhood.

CHAPTER 2

The Culture Clash

Where's Your Pants, Partner?

Sister Agatha was the "Mother Teresa" of DePaul Medical Center when I went to work there. Despite her advanced age she worked tirelessly to serve the sick, poor and dying in our community. I'm not Catholic, but I respected Sister Agatha for her ceaseless and passionate service to others.

After working on a few community projects with Sister Agatha's help, I invited her to my home for dinner. I never actually thought she would take me up on my offer, but I wanted to invite her anyway, to show my appreciation for her. To my surprise she did accept the invitation. When I told my wife later that day neither of us could have been prepared for the evening that was to unfold.

Sister Agatha (with another nun) arrived at our home right on time. At the time Emerson, my third son, was only three years old. We had a nice dinner and conversation, and the kids were all well mannered and even obedient. Things couldn't have been going better.

When eight o'clock rolled around I asked the kids to go upstairs to get ready for bed. They ran upstairs with an "okay dad" and disappeared. Imagine my pride. My kids were being model citizens. They were orderly and more than willing to obey their Mom and Dad, even at bedtime! Then it happened. My wife and I were having a nice conversation with the Sisters when Emerson appeared before us all—wearing only the tops to his pajamas!

What was I supposed to do? I'm not Catholic so I didn't know the proper protocol for this type of event. I had seen some television shows, but there was no confessional in my home! I didn't even have a Rosary! What would the Sisters think, or do? The focus immediately turned to me as the head of my household and I did what anyone would do, I guess.

I turned to my young son, smiled, and said very matter of factly, "Where's your pants, partner?" As he began to explain that he couldn't find his pajama bottoms my wife sprang into action and took him upstairs to get situated.

Emerson's complete innocence was disarming. He had no idea that coming downstairs pants-less might be inappropriate, and by God's grace the moment became another treasured memory.

In some ways, that's how our teens are today. They just don't know that what they're thinking or doing is in some way inappropriate. They're not necessarily trying to be proud, or rebellious—they truly think they have the savvy and experience to make their own decisions without their father's help—and often times they're right. On many other occasions, however, they think they can see clearly when in reality they are desperately shortsighted.

It's part of growing up. When you see your son attempting to make decisions independently, it's not necessarily rebellion. It may be his way of stretching out his wings in growing up. If we as dads can keep this in mind, understanding that our sons are changing into men just as God intended, we will be better equipped to respond with loving instruction instead of angry correction.

Why don't our sons know that they are naked? Why aren't the alarms going off in their heads and hearts? Remember, they're "growing up;" they're not "grown up." Their environment has been a huge influence on them and they have learned much from the culture that surrounds them.

So let's keep our boy's "rebellion" in perspective. Consider the patience, kindness, and mercy Jesus shows to each of us sinners as he draws us to himself. Even on the Cross, betrayed and rejected by the world, Jesus asked the Father to "Forgive them, for they know not what they do."

Let's show our sons the same patience, kindness and mercy. In so doing we will be showing them Christ and leading them by example to true biblical manhood.

The Culture Clash

In Matthew 13, Jesus describes a clash of cultures that existed when he walked the earth, and that he knew would become increasingly apparent as time went on.

> Jesus told them another parable: "The kingdom of heaven is like a man who sowed good seed in his field. But while everyone was sleeping, his enemy came and sowed weeds among the wheat, and went away. When the wheat sprouted and formed heads, then the weeds also appeared.
>
> The owner's servants came to him and said, 'Sir, didn't you sow good seed in your field? Where then did the weeds come from?'
>
> " 'An enemy did this,' he replied.
>
> "The servants asked him, 'Do you want us to go and pull them up?'
>
> " 'No,' he answered, 'because while you are pulling the weeds, you may root up the wheat with them. Let both grow together until the harvest. At that time I will tell the harvesters: First collect the weeds and tie them in bundles to be burned; then gather the wheat and bring it into my barn.' "
>
> —Matthew 13:24–30

The owner (God) of the field (the world) has decided to allow both the wheat (the children of God) and the weeds (the enemies of God) to live together, sharing the field until the harvest (Christ's return and judgment). Until Christ returns, the children of the kingdom will live in the world with the enemies of God, inhabiting the same soil but often times behaving differently and producing very different fruit.

Today, some two thousand years after Jesus spoke this parable, the crop has moved much further along toward maturity and the harvest. The competing cultures of the wheat and the weeds increasingly result in a clash between the kingdom of God and the ways and values of the world. The clash is played out every day in our schools, our media, our elections, and even in our homes. It's seen in the divide over abortion, over leadership, over sex education, over modesty, over the definition of marriage, and in many other issues and decisions that we constantly wrestle with as a society.

This is the culture your son is surrounded by on a daily basis—the culture of the weeds. It is a culture of continual hostility toward godliness, where the permanent job description of the weeds is to do everything possible to stunt, compromise, and choke out the life of the wheat.

Paul recognized this clash of cultures when he encouraged the Colossians to be rooted in Christ and to be aware of false philosophies that could work to deceive them.

> So then, just as you received Christ Jesus as Lord, continue to live in him, rooted and built up in him, strengthened in the faith as you were taught, and overflowing with thankfulness. See to it that no one takes you captive through hollow and deceptive philosophy, which depends on human tradition and the basic principles of this world rather than on Christ.
>
> —Colossians 2:6–8

This clash of cultures will only be fully resolved when Christ returns, but you can be encouraged that God has chosen your son to live in this culture at this time, for Christ's purposes. He has also given him a Christian father who cares enough about him to read books like this one. Right there, your son has a huge advantage. Ultimately it may not mean much unless you lead as God calls you to, but if you prepare your son for true manhood, then by God's grace he can flourish amidst this clash of cultures.

Truth and Discernment

When your son was quite young he had no real sense of the difference between right and wrong. He had no way to tell truth from lies, no way to discern the influence of the wheat from the influence of the weeds. How could he? The Bible teaches that we are all born following the desires of the sinful flesh. Our natural cravings are anything but godly, even from birth. Consequently, it is essential to understand that your son can never become the man God created him to be until he has a personal relationship with God through the finished work of Jesus Christ.

Now that your son is getting older, part of his maturation must and will include him taking greater initiative and increasingly making more important decisions on his own. As he matures it is quickly becoming his responsibility to discern things for himself. It's up to you to show him that becoming a true man depends on being changed by the regenerating work of the Spirit, to the glory of God.

How does a young man discern truth from lies? After all, sometimes there seems to be good arguments on both sides of an issue. Thankfully, in every area where it is imperative that we know truth, God has made truth available to us through his Word—the sword of the Spirit. It is upon this truth that this book relies, and it is upon this truth that you must rely if you are to effectively serve your son.

Deep in the Weeds

While visiting one of the leading bookstore chains recently, I asked a clerk to help me locate books on "Father-Son Talks." She knew exactly what I was referring to and led me straight to the teen section. There she pointed out about fifteen books and told me which ones she had used for her twelve-year-old son. These books on manhood were written for boys ages three to nineteen. Most were well written and seemed to be targeted to the teen reader. Some were illustrated in great detail while others used cartoon-like characters to depict the changing human form. Most did a good job of describing the human body and the anatomical changes of both boys and girls.

As I reviewed these books, one thing stood out to me. The concept of character was almost entirely missing, as if the ideas of "right and wrong" and "good and bad" simply don't apply to male maturation. In most cases morality was only mentioned in order to dismiss it as a topic of serious consideration. Right and wrong were portrayed as completely subjective. According to most of the books I reviewed, all a young man has to do to tell right from wrong is "look within" or "listen to his heart," and then "do what's right for him."

As I said, most of these books did get the anatomy right, but while anatomy is certainly integral to the discussion, it's the easy part. On a moral level it's also the least significant part of The Talk. The most significant part involves character. As we will discuss in greater detail in chapter 4, this book emphasizes six areas of character as being vital to true manhood and therefore central to The Talk: humility, courage, purity, faithfulness, self-lessness, and self-control.

Values like these were simply nowhere to be found in the volumes I took off the bookstore shelves that afternoon. Instead, portrayed as inevitable—or even held up as healthy and exemplary—were traits such as independence; sexual impurity and "experimentation"; self-centeredness; disregard for parental instruction; moral cowardice; and an ultimate disdain for any form of godliness. Here are some revealing quotes from books that represent secular culture's current take on what it means to become a man (the emphases in these quotes are mine):

"Accept that they [your parents] have the right to lay down some rules and try to agree on ones that you both can live with. Be willing to meet them halfway."[1]

"You owe it to yourself to listen to what your body and your emotions and your values are telling you."[2]

" . . . most of us realize that we aren't really mature enough to handle intercourse until at least our late teens . . . "[3]

"Is homosexuality morally wrong? In the past, many people felt that homosexuality was sinful or abnormal. There are still some people who feel this way. However, nowadays, more and more people no longer believe this. We feel that it's a personal matter, that some people happen to be homosexuals and that being homosexual is a perfectly healthy, normal, and acceptable way to be."[4]

"The Bible barely mentions homosexuality; our culture's great historical teaching book has much more to say about eating habits, for instance, than homosexuality."[5]

This is just the briefest glimpse at the material I found on the shelves that day. Imagine, this is what is given to our children to "help" them! Let's explore the content of the "moral instruction of the weeds" a bit further. Even if your son never sees these particular books, it's well worth taking a few more moments to help you understand what he will be up against without your active involvement.

You should know that the overwhelming majority of today's coming-of-age books for boys are written by women. It's not that I think women have nothing to say on the subject; it's just that men should have far more to say! It also speaks to the tendency of today's fathers to abdicate this responsibility.

Know also that the majority of these books are written to teens without any regard for their parents, much less the leadership of fathers. I recognize that in some families today neither parent provides any real leadership in helping a boy become a man. Even when there is little or no parental guidance, I'm convinced that most of these books do more harm than good. In some books, boys are not only encouraged to masturbate, they are encouraged to do so with other boys, or even with girls. One book I reviewed described homosexuality as normal, and encouraged boys to "experiment" in order to determine their "sexual preference."

These books generally teach that being a virtuous young man means little more than not getting a girl pregnant. Of course, if you do, according to these teen books there's a perfectly honorable backup plan: simply "terminate" the problem through abortion. Here are four points that I think accurately reflect the worldview of secular books written to guide a boy's transition into manhood.

1. God is irrelevant to the maturing process.
2. There is no such thing as a virtuous man.
3. It is healthy for boys to experiment with sexual indulgence and perversions.
4. Fathers are unnecessary to a son's moral development into manhood.

Alarmed? You should be. Am I overstating the case? Not at all. I implore you to take a walk down the aisles of your local bookstore and skim through the "coming of age" books—skipping over the anatomy sections—and in a few minutes you will see how bad it really is.

Teach from the Wheat

Imagine the tragedy of the well-intentioned father who chooses to entrust the moral education of his son to the culture of the weeds. I'll just get the boy a book, the father thinks, something written by a professional. God, however, didn't arrange for children to be born to professionals. He gives them to parents. Giving your son The Talk is not rocket science. You don't need a professional and you generally don't want a professional, at least not those who write the kind of books I just described. What you want and what you need is the faith and courage and commitment to serve your son in the grace and guidance God provides.

Thankfully, Scripture tells us clearly what it means to be wheat, not weeds. In the next two chapters we will discuss what true manhood looks like from Scripture so that you and your son might be "rooted and built up" in Christ.

CHAPTER 2 REVIEW

1. The culture your son lives in is one of continual hostility toward godliness, but God has chosen your son to live in this culture at this time, for Christ's purposes.
2. The worldview of most secular books written to guide a boy's transition into manhood is one of a blatant disregard for godliness. Instead they promote sexual experimentation, and a general disregard for parental instruction.
3. You don't need a professional to lead your son into true manhood. You need only the faith, courage and commitment to serve your son in the grace and guidance God provides.
4. When your son can't receive some information, or rebels against whole topics, be patient with him. Show the same love, mercy, and kindness that Christ continues to show to you, as you endeavor to love him and to be known by him.

CHAPTER 3

Manhood as Designed by God

A Charlie Brown Christmas

Is it just me or does Christmas roll around more quickly each year? Of course I would never get all caught up in the holiday. I make it a point of pride to always keep Christ at the center. Or do I?

My oldest son Stepheno was nine years old when I took him and my son Phillip, who was seven at the time, to get our Christmas tree. Walking through a makeshift fence we entered a nearby Christmas-tree lot and into a winter wonderland of sweet-smelling pines. I could see as we entered that there was a wide array of trees: Scotch Pines with their sharp bristly needles; long soft-needled White Pines, the classic Douglas and Fraser Firs, even a majestic Blue Spruce or two stood amidst the Christmas forest.

I knew exactly what I was looking for. I was, after all, an experienced Christmas tree hunter. As a teen I had worked one

Christmas season on a tree lot up in Northern Ohio, so I knew my pines.

As we entered the display area there was a small three-foot tree that had been put aside, presumably for disposal or donation, but it was the first tree my boys saw. "How about this one?" I joked as I walked on without a second glance.

As I got to the "real trees" I turned to see my boys examining the Charlie Brown tree. "Come on guys, look at this tree," I said, standing up a seven-foot Scotch Pine in an attempt to draw their attention away from the dying twig.

"We like this one," Stepheno said bluntly.

Now I'm all for inexpensive Christmas trees, but not that one! I'm not sure it even qualified as a Christmas tree. The few needles that clung to the branches would certainly be on the floor before Christmas rolled around. Not only that, but my wife was expecting a nice tree to decorate our home with for the season. She would certainly think I was the cheapest dad since the Grinch if I brought that tree home.

"Yeah, that is a nice tree, but let's look at a few others before we make a final decision," I suggested, and the boys finally relented and came to my side. I pulled up tree after tree trying to appeal to their senses. "Look how full this one is." "Look how tall that one is." "This one's so big that the star will touch the ceiling." I even played the Mom card suggesting that, "Mom would really like this one."

Finally, Stepheno turned to me, looked me square in the face and taught me a real Christmas lesson that I had forgotten. He simply said, "Dad, it doesn't matter how big the tree is."

He was right. His vision was 20/20 and mine—well, I had been nearsighted. The size, cost, and type of tree was completely irrelevant. This was the tree my boys loved, despite the fact that it had no outward appearance to attract me. It was not stately or grand by any means. It was humble and unmajestic—like my Savior.

I stood for a moment speechless as the truth of the moment washed over me. My arguments for "this tree" or "that tree" fell like so many pine needles to the forest floor. One by one each of my arguments entered my mind and each of them were undone—I stood corrected. I paid the five dollars for the tree and we headed home.

My wife greeted us at the door as my boys proudly marched up with prize in hand. I could see the doubt as her eyes moved from the tree to catch my gaze. Raising my eyebrows I said in hinting fashion, "This is the tree THE BOYS picked out, isn't it GREAT!"

My wife, being far more discerning than I, turned on a dime and welcomed the "beautiful" tree into our home, and I later explained the process by which it had been chosen. In hindsight we both agree that this small, frail tree was probably the best Christmas tree we will ever have.

God has put in each of us a desire to know him, to love him, to hear his voice, no matter our age or maturity. That Christmas my boys understood better than I that Christmas isn't about things, it is about relationship—our relationship with our Savior.

This is an important lesson to keep in mind as we proceed with The Talk. We have been made in the image of God, to be known by God, and to commune with him. As you will see, our relationship with God has profound implications when it comes to being a man.

Manhood as Designed by God

God is glorious and his creation, us included, was made to reflect his glory. Think about it: God consciously created us and this world to be a reflection of his very majesty. He also made a fantastic, sinless, glorious place for us to dwell.

Unfortunately, we allowed sin to enter the world and have been watching the world become increasingly corrupt ever since. But God did not stop there. He had a plan to redeem the world through his Son, our Savior, Jesus.

41

We have been granted the opportunity to be made anew in God's image. But what does that mean and what does this have to do with being a man? Let's take a look.

Before the world had been tainted by sin, "God created man in his own image, in the image of God he created him; male and female he created them" (Genesis 1:27). Here we have the clearest picture of man as he was made to be, a created being who in some sense displays the image of the ever-existing, uncreated God.

To understand manhood as God designed it, we need to appreciate what it means for a man to be created in God's image. For one thing, how could we as males be made in God's own image if he created them male and female, each one equally in that same image?

We have to begin by recognizing that our Father God is not flesh like us. Jesus himself explained that, "God is spirit, and his worshipers must worship in spirit and in truth" (John 4:24). If God is spirit and we are flesh, then being "made in his image" clearly does not mean that we physically resemble God.

From Genesis 2:7 we learn that, "the Lord God formed the man from the dust of the ground and breathed into his nostrils the breath of life, and the man became a living being." When man was first formed from the clay, he was not yet alive, but when the Lord breathed into that clay shape, it was given life and then a name: Adam.

We see from this verse that we are made in God's image spiritually, not physically.

This has important implications for our character and manner of living, as we will see in the following chapter. For now, however, let's return to the Garden and look at the "task list" God gave to this spiritual being called Adam, newly created in God's own image. Why is this important? Because it's the same "task list" God gives to us and to our sons. So that Adam would honorably represent God in the world, God called him to apply himself in four areas: his work, his sexual activity, his leadership in the home, and his obedience to God's law. Let's take a closer look at each of these.

The Cultural Mandate

Then God said, "Let us make man in our image, in our likeness, and let them rule over the fish of the sea and the birds of the air, over the livestock, over all the earth, and over all the creatures that move along the ground."

So God created man in his own image, in the image of God he created him; male and female he created them.

God blessed them and said to them, "Be fruitful and increase in number; fill the earth and subdue it. Rule over the fish of the sea and the birds of the air and over every living creature that moves on the ground."

—Genesis 1:26–28

Genesis 1:26–28 is often referred to as the Cultural or Creation Mandate. That is to say, what God "mandated" or commanded us to do when we were first created. We have been commanded to work, procreate, care for our family, and obey God.

Before we discuss these tasks it is important that we understand why we have been created. Understanding the "why" will help to keep us from straying into legalism when approaching these God-given tasks.

The first question of the Westminster Catechism is, "What is the chief end of man?" The answer is "to glorify God and to enjoy him forever." That means that the only way that we can fulfill our God-given tasks is to enter into each of them with a passion to glorify God that results in a distinct joy that comes from serving him with all of our heart, mind, soul and strength.

Only when we do our tasks in order to glorify God instead of trying to satisfy our own needs and desires can we confidently approach our task list knowing that each of our accomplishments have glorified God, and our joy has been made complete. Our heart attitude is what counts, not the doing in and of itself. How we do our tasks reflects our faith and our love for our Savior.

God designed us for joy and pleasure as much as he did for work. Like our work, this pleasure must be directed at finding

43

joy in God and not in the desires of our flesh. We are to do every-thing for the glory of God, and in so doing we find our greatest joy both in this world and the next.

This means that if you can't compete in a sport or leisure activity for the glory of God then you should not compete in that sport at all. If you cannot work for the glory of God then you need to examine your heart. God even wants your sons to have sex for the glory of God, and there is only one way to do that—in marriage. Sex is supposed to be pleasurable and fun, but only if it is done for God's glory.

Because we have been created expressly to glorify God and to enjoy him forever, everything we do should work to that end. As we glorify God in the tasks that he has prepared for us to do, the result will be the greatest joy and satisfaction in our work life, our sex life, our family life, and our spiritual life. With this understanding in mind, let's take a look at what your son needs to know about the tasks he has been given to accomplish.

Work

> The Lord God made the earth and the heavens—and no shrub of the field had yet appeared on the earth and no plant of the field had yet sprung up, for the Lord God had not sent rain on the earth and there was no man to work the ground.
> —Genesis 2:4–5

In this passage we see two things. First, even before man was created, it was God's intention for him to work. Second, we see that according to God's order of things, an essential role for man is to be a worker.

Adam, who represented all mankind, was given the two-fold task of working the garden and caring for all that was in it. "The Lord God took the man and put him in the Garden of Eden to work it and take care of it" (Genesis 2:15). This is the first duty of man before the fall: to work.

Your son needs to see that taking on the responsibilities of work is an important part of gradually transitioning from boy to man.

There is a place for fun and rest but we are commanded to work. God himself models the pattern of work and rest, as seen in Genesis 2:2–3. As for us, we are granted rest from our work. We are not commanded to play video games, or watch movies, or play sports, or go hunting or fishing—although there is nothing wrong with these things when we use them to glorify God. God commands us to be diligent and productive workers before we are granted rest. We should delight in our work as it brings glory to God and reflects our love for our Savior. This is one of the cornerstone points of The Talk, and one we will discuss in more detail in chapter 13.

Sex

> God blessed them and said to them, "Be fruitful and increase in number; fill the earth and subdue it." . . . a man will leave his father and mother and be united to his wife, and they will become one flesh.
>
> —Genesis 1:28, 2:24 (NIV)

God is not shy in letting us know that we have been created to be sexually active. He always intended us to be fulfilled sexually, so he set sexual pleasure into a single righteous and blameless framework: marriage. From the moment of her creation, Eve was Adam's wife, and it is within the context of heterosexual marriage that God has given us the ability to fulfill the righteous, joyful, and holy act of sexual intercourse.

Clearly, Adam and Eve are actually encouraged to have sex in order to procreate, but only in as much as they are able to glorify God in their sexual relationship. God calls us to only have sex within the context of marriage. He also calls us to love our wives as he loves the church, with an unselfish and sacrificial love. The same is true for our sons. God expects them to be righteous and holy in their sexual relations. We are to think of our spouse's needs and pleasure before our own, caring for her and sacrificing our own desires for hers.

When we glorify God in our sexual relations we are safe from guilt and harm; we are able to enjoy sex fully; and God is pleased.

This complex and pervasive subject will be addressed further in several additional chapters.

Family

> For Adam no suitable helper was found. So the LORD God caused the man to fall into a deep sleep; and while he was sleeping, he took one of the man's ribs and closed up the place with flesh. Then the LORD God made a woman from the rib he had taken out of the man, and he brought her to the man.
>
> —Genesis 2:20–22

In explicitly creating Eve for Adam, God established a permanent order within the human social framework. Adam was to lead and care for Eve, and Eve was to be Adam's helper. This does not suggest a lower position; God is clear that he made Adam and Eve equally in his image. The difference between them lies in their roles.

Listen to what God said when he reprimanded Adam. "Because you listened to your wife and ate from the tree about which I commanded you, 'You must not eat of it' " (Genesis 3:17). Here God reminds Adam that he was commanded to glorify God by leading and caring for his wife, Eve. Adam should have not only obeyed God's command; he should have protected his wife. Leading and caring: both were Adam's responsibility, both are your responsibility, and both will be your son's responsibility when he is married. We will discuss marriage in more detail in chapter 15.

Obedience

> And the Lord God commanded the man, "You are free to eat from any tree in the garden; but you must not eat from the tree of the knowledge of good and evil, for when you eat of it you will surely die."
>
> —Genesis 2:16–17

Did you know that God's law existed before the fall and even before the creation of woman? It was simple, but also very clear— Adam was called to honor God through his obedience. He failed.

How many clear and simple commands have you failed to obey recently? How about these?

- Do not let any unwholesome talk come out of your mouths, but only what is helpful for building others up according to their needs, that it may benefit those who listen (Ephesians 4:29).
- Be joyful always; pray continually; give thanks in all circumstances, for this is God's will for you in Christ Jesus (1 Thessalonians 5:16–18).
- Each one of you also must love his wife as he loves himself (Ephesians 5:33).

Even though Adam and Eve's hearts were sinless prior to the fall, they were still tempted through the craftiness of the serpent. They chose to disobey God, though their hearts were sinless and pure. How easy it is for you, me, and our sons—who are all born with sinful hearts—to fall into temptation!

So what do we do about this? If it is so easy to fail God, and he has given us these four arenas—work, sex, family, and obedience—in which to follow him, what should we say to our sons about how to live? The answer begins with understanding the basic virtues of manhood, and what it means to pursue them in a way that honors God. That is the subject of our next chapter.

CHAPTER 3 REVIEW

1. So that Adam would honorably represent God in the world, God called him to apply himself in four areas: his work, his sexual activity, his leadership in the home, and his obedience to God's law. God's call to you and your son is the same.
2. Man's first duty before the fall was to work—working and caring for the things God put before him.
3. God has designed us to be sexually active, within the protective boundaries of marriage.

4. God has called your son to be a godly leader of his home, loving and caring for his wife.
5. We are dependent upon the finished work of Jesus Christ to save us from our sin and empower us to live a holy and godly life.

CHAPTER 4

The Virtues of Manhood

A s we have seen, our calling in God—your son's calling—will be carried out in the arenas of work, sex, family, and obedience to God's commands. We do this as creatures made in the image of God. That is, we resemble God in that we are spiritual beings. That's why Scripture teaches us to be holy and blameless, putting on spiritual attributes and putting off worldly ones. We are called to grow in holiness so that we might become more and more like our holy God, who is Spirit, not flesh.

I'm a Poacher!

It was a warm spring day and I sat working behind my desk. I had been to an event a few days earlier and had won a BB gun that I gave to my son as a present. Along with the gun came clear and detailed instructions on how and when it could be used.

The phone rang and I picked it up to hear my son Stepheno crying on the other end. "Stepheno? What's wrong?" I asked as my heart began pounding. I had never received a call like this before, and I knew something had to be very wrong.

Stepheno started in a halting, almost undecipherable sob, "Dad, I didn't mean to . . . I didn't think it would shoot that far . . . I'm sorry . . . I didn't mean it."

By now the sobs were making complete sentences indiscernible and I began using the scant pieces of information to paint a picture of what had happened in my mind. It had something to do with the BB gun. He shot his brother Phillip, or maybe Emerson with it, but it wasn't too close and it appeared that Mom wasn't home, or she was taking him to the hospital. My mind immediately shifted into panic gear.

"Stepheno," I replied rather sternly, "slow down and stop crying. I can't understand you. Now tell me what happened."

He tried to slow down, but instead of adding details his sobs filled all the voids. "I . . . took the BB gun and . . . I didn't know it would shoot that far. I really didn't know, I didn't even pump it up all the way," and the sobs broke out again.

"Stepheno, who did you shoot? Who did you shoot with the BB gun?" I asked as calmly as I could. My heart was racing now and I was already berating myself for ever giving him the gun in the first place. He must have shot Phillip, but was he okay? Were they in need of help? "Oh my God help us!" I thought as I awaited his response. "Stepheno, tell me who you shot!"

"It was . . . sob . . . a dove, but it was all the way to the woods and I shot him from the bathroom window. I didn't mean it! . . . I didn't know that the gun would shoot that far, I'M A POACHER!" he exclaimed bursting out in tears again.

Relief swept through me like a head wind over the bow of a ship. In a split second I went from trying to hide my panic to trying to hide my laughter. I thought he had shot one of my other children only to find out he had shot a bird, and accidentally at that. What a tender heart, what conviction, what power!

Stepheno was undone by the conviction that he had done something wrong. He wasn't scared of the consequence that I might bring, but rather what the incident itself had made him . . . a poacher.

When I got home I walked my son through the implications of his poor decision to use the BB gun without permission. He was appropriately disciplined, but my primary concern was to guard the spiritual seed within him that brought such strong and powerful conviction.

We all need to understand our relationship with God and how that relationship dictates the man we will, or will not, be. You need to teach your son how to discern the voice of God's Spirit and how to respond to that small still voice. It is that very voice of love, mercy and kindness that we can somehow find ourselves at odds with when we are tempted.

Your young man needs convictions and they can't come from you. Convictions come from hearing the voice of the Lord. They come from having a holy fear of God and knowing in your heart of hearts his will for you. Convictions allow a man to steady his walk in order to stay on the narrow road that leads to life.

To be able to hear the voice of the Lord, discern his will in your life, and to act upon it in a way that brings him glory is everything you need to be a true man.

Putting Off, Putting On

As Paul wrote to the Ephesians, "Praise be to the God and Father of our Lord Jesus Christ, who has blessed us in the heavenly realms with every spiritual blessing in Christ. For he chose us in him before the creation of the world to be holy and blameless in his sight" (Ephesians 1:3–4). Then he added,

> You were taught, with regard to your former way of life, to **put off** your old self, which is being corrupted by its deceitful desires; to **be made new in the attitude of your minds**; and to **put on** the new self, **created to be like God in true righteousness and holiness.**
> —Ephesians 4:21–24

How can we—creatures who are physical and spiritual and fallen in our sin—obey this verse? How can we triumph over our sin and our flesh to perform this profoundly spiritual act? More to the point of this book, if you and I have a hard enough time trying to obey this verse, how can your immature young son accomplish this?

Simple answer: Your son's spiritual victories will have the same origin as every one of your spiritual victories. To rise above the temptations of the world your son must set his mind on the things of the Spirit. Scripture teaches us to put to death those thoughts and desires that are of the earthly nature and to begin to show evidence of our new spiritual nature that is "being renewed in knowledge in the image of its creator."

> Put to death, therefore, whatever belongs to your earthly nature: sexual immorality, impurity, lust, evil desires and greed, which is idolatry. Because of these, the wrath of God is coming. You used to walk in these ways, in the life you once lived. But now you must rid yourselves of all such things as these: anger, rage, malice, slander, and filthy language from your lips. Do not lie to each other, since you have taken off your old self with its practices and have put on the new self, which is being renewed in knowledge in the image of its Creator. Here there is no Greek or Jew, circumcised or uncircumcised, barbarian, Scythian, slave or free, but Christ is all, and is in all.
>
> Therefore, as God's chosen people, holy and dearly loved, clothe yourselves with compassion, kindness, humility, gentleness and patience. Bear with each other and forgive whatever grievances you may have against one another. Forgive as the Lord forgave you. And over all these virtues put on love, which binds them all together in perfect unity.
>
> —Colossians 3:5–14

We have been made in God's image. We have the amazing privilege of being spiritual beings, just as God is a spiritual being. The responsibility that comes with that privilege (privilege and responsibility always go together) is that we are called to pursue spiritual growth. We are called to become ever more "like God in true righteousness and holiness." This pursuit is the essence of honorable manhood, even honorable young manhood.

That's a daunting project, isn't it? Does it seem impossible? As impossible as, I don't know, a camel squeezing through the eye of a needle? If that's how you see it, you're on the right track. Not only that, but you're in the right place to be able to communicate this truth accurately to your son. For our Savior told us that, "with man this is impossible, but with God all things are possible" (Matthew 19:26).

Here's the challenge your son needs to understand. Like Adam, we are required to be perfectly blameless and completely holy in our obedience to God. The problem, of course, is that none of us ever do this perfectly. As James said, "We all stumble in many ways" (James 3:2). So if we are sure to fail from time to time, yet God calls us to be perfectly holy, what does it mean to walk as a man before God? It means that we must put our trust completely in the finished work of Jesus Christ, who alone can make us holy and pure. It means that when we stumble and fall short of the glory of God we do two things. First, we return to the Lord and ask him for forgiveness, genuinely repentant yet confident that this specific sin we just committed was a sin Christ died to forgive. Second, we pick ourselves up again and keep going, continually seeking to obey God by the power of his grace. This is the basis of all repentance: turning away from our sin and in our love of God heading in the opposite direction, back to him again and again.

This is where our degree of familiarity and our current experience with God's Word becomes crucial. Through the Bible we learn and are reminded of what God commands of us, and we recall the power and love and grace he offers us for both obedience and forgiveness. This means we should be continually growing in our knowledge of God through his Word. The Psalmist certainly got it right when he wrote, "How can a young man keep his way pure? By living according to your Word. I seek you with all my heart; do not let me stray from your commands. I have hidden your word in my heart that I might not sin against you" (Psalm 119:9–11).

The Metrics of Manhood

So then, we are spiritual creatures. We are made in God's image. We are called by his grace to live in perfect holiness before him, and when we fail we can look to Christ for forgiveness and fresh grace. How then can we measure our progress, our success? How can we know we are becoming more like God in righteousness and true holiness? Actually, it's not that difficult. As we press on toward this goal our growth can be readily seen in the virtues, or character traits, that rise to the surface. What virtues should we aim for? What do we want our sons to be like?

Let's start with a definition of manhood that is currently popular in much of western culture. According to this definition, a "real man" can be described something like this:

- Muscular and athletic
- Never overweight
- Definitely not an acne sufferer
- A rugged individualist who answers only to himself
- A person who is tolerant of everyone and everything, because there are no absolutes in his life, only opinions
- Open to many views of morality, truth, and right and wrong
- A ladies' man, with the emphasis on the plural, even if his choice in "ladies" is another man
- Basically deserving of anything he might want or desire
- Focused on being (or at least appearing to be) wealthy, smart, accepted, talented, liked, and admired

Is this the kind of man you hope your boy will become? Are these the "virtues" you want to see manifested in his life? I doubt it. In Galatians 5:19–21 Paul describes the natural tendency of our sinful nature to lead us into "sexual immorality, impurity

54

and debauchery; idolatry and witchcraft; hatred, discord, jealousy, fits of rage, selfish ambition, dissensions, factions and envy; drunkenness, orgies, and the like."

Paul then contrasts these detestable things of our sinful nature with the fruit of the Spirit of God in Galatians 5:22–23. "But the fruit of the Spirit is love, joy, peace, patience, kindness, goodness, faithfulness, gentleness and self-control."

I believe we can distill from Scripture six virtues to use as benchmarks and goals, things we can hold onto, measure, evaluate, and work to improve as we mature. It is not my intention to make an airtight case for these six being the only possible choices. Certainly there are other virtues that can be identified in Scripture. My goal here—especially as you prepare to talk with your young son—is to keep it simple by providing a biblically solid list that is easy to remember and will point your son in the right direction. A biblical description of a real man is as follows. A real man is:

- Humble
- Courageous
- Morally pure
- Faithful
- Selfless
- Self-controlled

How well do these terms line up with that first set of bullet points—the worldly view of a man? Not a lot of overlap, is there? Where is the self-centeredness, self-seeking, and self-glorification that the world continually emphasizes? Where are the themes of consumption and indulgence? Where is the sense of entitlement? In their place, we see a striking emphasis on looking outward. The second set of bullet points describe a man who takes the attitude of a servant toward others, whose life is focused not on self-exaltation but on glorifying God with his life. The world's version of a man essentially sees others as raw material for his own gratification and glorification. The true man, on the other hand, according to God's definition, seeks to love his neighbor and to consider others as better than himself.

Six Key Virtues for Men

These six virtues are spiritual fruit, closely and directly associated with being like God in true righteousness and holiness. The more we become like God, the more these virtues will be evident in us. For each virtue there is a short definition and a few verses for emphasis and elaboration. Paying close attention to these virtues will help you set your sights on exactly where you want to lead your son.

Humility

To pursue humility means choosing to accept the fact that your knowledge and abilities are limited, and in light of that, you are regularly seeking help and graciously receiving advice and correction.

- This is the one I esteem: he who is humble and contrite in spirit, and trembles at my word (Isaiah 66:2).
- All of you, clothe yourselves with humility toward one another, because, God opposes the proud but gives grace to the humble (1 Peter 5:5).
- Humility and the fear of the LORD bring wealth and honor and life (Proverbs 22:4).

Courage

To pursue courage means choosing to do what is right despite the opposition of others or of your own desires (often the more difficult enemy to fight).

- Be on your guard; stand firm in the faith; be men of courage; be strong (1 Corinthians 16:13).

- So keep up your courage, men, for I have faith in God that it will happen just as he told me (Acts 27:25).
- Act with courage, and may the LORD be with those who do well. (2 Chronicles 19:11)

Purity

To pursue moral purity means choosing to live by the highest moral principles in both speech and physical relations, despite your own desires to do otherwise, and despite any external pressure to compromise.

- How can a young man keep his way pure? By living according to your word (Psalm 119:9).
- Treat younger men as brothers, older women as mothers, and younger women as sisters, with absolute purity (1 Timothy 5:1–2).
- Set an example for the believers in speech, in life, in love, in faith and in purity (1 Timothy 4:12).
- Do not be hasty in the laying on of hands, and do not share in the sins of others. Keep yourself pure (1 Timothy 5:22).

Faithfulness

To pursue faithfulness means acting in integrity, keeping your word, and doing what is right before God, with fortitude and without complaint, because you trust God to give you the ability to complete all he has given you to do.

- So then, men ought to regard us as servants of Christ and as those entrusted with the secret things of God. Now it is required that those who have been given a trust must prove faithful (1 Corinthians 4:1–2).
- Love the LORD, all his saints! The LORD preserves the faithful, but the proud he pays back in full. Be strong and take heart, all you who hope in the LORD (Psalm 31:23–24).
- A faithful man will be richly blessed (Proverbs 28:20).

Selflessness

To pursue selflessness means placing the well-being of others before your own needs and desires.

- An unfriendly man pursues selfish ends; he defies all sound judgment (Proverbs 18:1).
- Do nothing out of selfish ambition or vain conceit, but in humility consider others better than yourselves. Each of you should look not only to your own interests, but also to the interests of others (Philippians 2:3–4).
- For where you have envy and selfish ambition, there you find disorder and every evil practice (James 3:16).

Self-control

To pursue self-control means to live according to the Spirit of God, choosing to glorify God with our lives and deny the sinful nature when tempted to do otherwise.

- Be self-controlled and alert. Your enemy the devil prowls around like a roaring lion looking for someone to devour (1 Peter 5:8).
- Like a city whose walls are broken down is a man who lacks self-control (Proverbs 25:28).
- But the fruit of the Spirit is love, joy, peace, patience, kindness, goodness, faithfulness, gentleness and self-control. Against such things there is no law (Galatians 5:22–23).

We All Need Help

When society settles on a false definition of what is good and desirable in a man, the streets become full of males who have never grown into biblical manhood. Guys like these might look cool, but morally they may be little more than children. What a sad and tragic thing that so many boys today fall into this trap and never get out! They buy into the world's definition of manhood and end up going to their graves morally stunted. The externals of chasing this worldly definition of manhood—things like sexual conquests, shiny new cars, and rugged good looks—can never qualify anyone for true manhood.

Your son doesn't have to become a man like that. He has you to help him, and you have Christ, the Word of God, and fellow believers to help you.

The truth is that we all need help. Being a man is a daunting task, impossible on your own. To become more like Christ in true righteousness and holiness, a man's mind must be renewed and his heart must be regenerated. In short, your son needs divine intervention, and you must remind him of his dependence on God and the regenerating work of Jesus Christ. For your son to be the man that he was created to be requires full and complete reliance on Jesus Christ.

It is in these God-given, God-empowered virtues that your talk with your son should be wrapped. I guarantee these are not character traits or choices that have been discussed with your son at a public school. They are rarely seen on television or in the movies. If you want to be sure your son has an understanding of what it means to be a man, you will most likely need to be the one to tell him. In any event, you are far and away the best one to tell him.

CHAPTER 4 REVIEW

1. Your son's spiritual victories will have the same origin as every one of your spiritual victories. He must learn to trust solely in the finished work of Jesus Christ. Without a relationship with Christ it is impossible to walk in the holiness required to be the man God has called him to be.
2. Scripturally, a real man is humble, courageous, morally pure, faithful, selfless, and self-controlled. Your talk with your son should continually emphasize these God-given, God-empowered virtues.

3. It is in these God-given, God-empowered virtues (humility, courage, purity, faithfulness, selflessness, and self-control) that your talk with your son should be wrapped.
4. Scriptural manhood means hearing the Lord's voice, discerning his will for your life, and acting upon it in a way that brings glory to God.

CHAPTER 5

Planning "The Talk"

This chapter will help you know when your son is ready for The Talk. It will give you guidelines for planning the location, preparing your son, and setting goals.

Slam Dunk

I couldn't understand why I had such a difficult time talking to my boys. I gave them the time. I even gave them solid instruction. What was wrong with them? I'm their father after all and certainly they know that I only want what's best for them! I was stumped until I took my son out for dinner after one of his varsity basketball games. I was tired and hungry so I sat and ate while he did the talking. We talked about the game and the role he played. I listened, adding a comment here and there when I was invited to do so. Before long he began to turn the conversation to the things I had been trying to talk to him about, only now he was willing and able to converse. He was actually leading the conversation.

What I didn't realize is that I had been giving him my time, on my terms, and on my turf. It wasn't the proper soil to plant the seed I was trying to grow—the seed of helping a teen learn to be a man and begin to walk on his own. He didn't need or want the training wheels anymore.

Now I take my sons out one-on-one as often as I have opportunity. After games, plays, presentations, on our way home from school, or where ever. I find that if I take the time and I don't press the conversations, that he really wants to talk to me about most things. Sometimes I need to spend extra time so that the inconsequential conversation has time to die down and the important stuff has opportunity to rise to the top. I have to remember that it's about being available at the right times, not making the time when you're available.

This is an important lesson for us dads to learn. Proverbs 18:13 says that "He who answers before listening—that is his folly and his shame." Verse 15 follows up saying that "The heart of the discerning acquires knowledge; the ears of the wise seek it out." So let's be wise dads. Begin acquiring knowledge about your son right now, no matter how young he is, by making it a priority to spend time with him—just him and dad. More importantly, make it a point to acquire knowledge by determining now to listen first and speak later.

All this time I had been shooting air balls and I couldn't figure out why. Now, almost by chance, I was putting down some slam dunks! The reason? Life's slam dunks begin to happen as we become true servants of those under our authority. In Mark 10:42–45, Jesus tells his disciples that unlike the thinking of worldly leaders, whoever wants to become truly great must become the servant of all. Following Christ means that you become a servant just like he did. "For even the Son of Man did not come to be served, but to serve, and to give his life as a ransom for many."

For your son this means taking the time to be with him, to listen to him, to really consider his thoughts as important, and most importantly, not to "lord it over him."

By the way, this is equally important for you dads with daughters, so start making individual time for all your children at the earliest possible ages. If you can focus on listening it will be both fun and informative.

Times and Seasons

Discerning when to give The Talk to your son doesn't have to be difficult or full of uncertainty. There are indications that will usually tell you whether he is ready, and how much he may be ready to hear. In fact, tailoring your presentation of The Talk to the maturity, knowledge level, and temperament of your son is one of the most effective things a wise father can do for his boy. Each time I have given The Talk to one of my sons, I have done it a little differently, always with the goal of helping that particular young man really hear what the Lord is saying to him.

For example, when my oldest son was eleven, I began asking him general questions about the changes his body might be going through. I was trying to gauge what had taken place and how he was responding. Based on his answers it was obvious that some of these topics were completely new to him, while others were familiar. This told me that although he was not ready for The Talk in all its detail, it was clearly time to introduce the subject.

I strongly encourage you to begin some initial discussion of these topics with your son before his hormones begin to kick in at full force. When you take that approach, The Talk will tend to come in stages, starting at perhaps age ten or eleven. Some young men may not hear it all until age fifteen or sixteen, and that's okay. Many fathers and sons find it easier and more comfortable to take a step-by-step approach, which is really the way we learn most things, isn't it?

Boys who are given their first exposure to The Talk at age eleven have usually finished The Talk by thirteen or fourteen. Some boys may reach fifteen or even sixteen before you have given them all the details of The Talk. However, if your son gets to age sixteen and you two still have not had The Talk to any significant degree, perhaps your discernment needs evaluation. It is possible your son may not be ready, but it's much more likely that you don't know him as well as you think, or are simply putting off what you see as an unpleasant task.

Here are some of the signs that can help you determine when your son is probably ready for an initial Talk. Some of these signs will be obvious to you. Others you will need to ask about. In either case, discussing these changes can offer you a relatively easy conversation path that leads in a clear direction.

Physical changes
- Underarm hair
- Facial hair
- Pubic hair and erections
- Muscular development
- Voice that cracks or deepens
- Increased sweating
- Acne or pimples
- Growth spurts

Changes in behavior or influences
- Increased interest in girls
- Significant input from TV, movies, or questionable internet use
- Increased unguarded time with boys his age or older
- Evidence of being familiar with adult themes
- Increased time spent alone in bedroom or bathroom

Is He Ready?

When you recognize two or three of these signs, it's time to ask some simple questions, trying to be as unthreatening as you can.[1]

Asking about underarm hair, for example, may gain you little information for discerning timing, but it's a no-risk way of broaching the subject of manhood. So ask him about this and other changes he may have recognized in his body. (Chapter 7 offers a refresher course on anatomical changes if your memory is a bit hazy.) If he doesn't respond with anything substantial, try more specific questions. "Have you experienced any changes in and around your penis? As boys get older they begin to have erections. That means your penis gets hard and straight. Have you had that happen to you yet?"

Don't expect your son's answers to be forthright at this point. Boys are typically shy about discussing these things, and for most fathers this will be the first time you have had such a frank discussion with your son. So watch his reactions. If he is shy or quiet, then most likely he has had an erection but isn't comfortable talking about it yet. Pursue the topic a little further in a way that is reassuring. "Erections are part of being a man and while it is a personal subject, there is nothing to be ashamed of."

If, on the other hand, you detect a certain unbelief or incredulity, then perhaps he is truly unaware of these things. In this case, simply reassure him that such changes are normal and that you will be talking to him more about manhood in the near future.

Keep in mind that in having this first test-the-waters conversation, you are opening a line of communication and not simply planning a one-time discussion of "man stuff." This is the beginning of a new season in your relationship, so take Paul's advice to heart: "Be completely humble and gentle; be patient, bearing with one another in love. Make every effort to keep the unity of the Spirit through the bond of peace" (Ephesians 4:2–3). It will take time and probably quite a few conversations to build this new dimension of your relationship. For now, you are just gauging if the time is right to open the discussion and you are humbly, gently trying to be an encouragement to your son.

In your first set of questions (remember, this is before The Talk officially begins), here are some points you should make clear to your son:

- If he hasn't experienced all these things yet, they're on the way
- These changes continue for a number of years
- Every boy experiences these changes as they get older
- Your son can come talk to you about these changes at any time and you will always tell him the truth
- You will be discussing these things with him in more detail
- Wisdom and all the answers to these questions and issues are found in the Bible

Location, Location, Location

Once you have determined that the time is right for an initial Talk, the next step is to arrange for an appropriate venue. There are many places and settings that can work effectively, as long as a few key points are considered.

First, be sure the place you choose will offer a relaxing, non-threatening, and interruption-proof environment. Your son needs to be able to grasp the significance of this time with his dad. He needs to be someplace he can pay close attention to your instruction, with few or no distractions. He needs to be put at the greatest ease possible, freeing him to ask questions and inquire of things he had not dared to mention before.

The right location can depend a lot on your son. For my oldest boy, we just took a walk in the woods on a warm fall afternoon. I found a place a mile or so from any homes, cars, or people. We sat on some fallen trees, surrounded by forest, and for the next three hours we talked about manhood. My son loves the outdoors and we have spent many hours outside working, riding dirt bikes, or just walking and talking. It was natural for us to be there. It was relaxing, isolated, and certainly non-intimidating. Here are some ideas that might work for you and your son.

Local Retreats

How about a nearby hotel? Arrive early enough to take advantage of the facilities. Go for a swim, play tennis or racquetball, and have a good dinner. When you make your reservation, ask that the television be removed from your room before you check in, as its presence would almost certainly be a distraction. It may seem strange, but any hotel worthy of your business will remove the television without question. You can begin The Talk at dinner and move into the more sensitive topics when you return to your room.

Road Trips

Consider taking your son on a road trip to a favorite event. Make it something big-league. It can be football, NASCAR, golf, or a symphony—as long as it will be a thrill to your son and acceptable to you. The time on the road is a good place to begin to draw your son out, but not a place to actually have The Talk. One caution: only choose this option if you can separate the excitement and distraction of the entertainment from what is really the main event: The Talk itself.

Camping or Fishing

Getting out in the woods, to places no one else is likely to be, usually provides a fun and acceptable setting. I know many men whose fondest memories of their father are from hunting or camping trips. Some of the most intimate discussions with my sons have taken place in a duck blind in the quiet of the early morning. These are times none of us will ever forget.

Men's Day at Home

While it does take a little extra planning and discipline, it can work just fine to have The Talk in your own home. First, you need to make sure everyone else will be out of the house. You might have to give mom and sister an excuse to be away for four hours or longer. It is best if you can send the rest of the family away overnight. Order pizza or any of your son's favorite foods to set the right mood and avoid having to prepare anything. Be sure to turn off the ringers on all phones, disconnect the answering machine, and shut down every electronic distraction and every computer in the house. Let your son know that you will not entertain any interruptions.

Maintain Focus

This insistence on blocking out all conceivable interruptions is a rule that should be applied to The Talk in every possible way. You must do everything you can to keep this time sacred. Your son must recognize that this time is your absolute top priority, so important to you that, in a day when many of us are often trying to do several things at once, you have ruthlessly eliminated all possible distractions so that your full attention can be given to your son. If you can't do that, then even though your son may be completely ready for The Talk, I would have to say that you are not.

This will mean no cell phones, no pagers, no laptops, and no PDA alarms. At an absolute minimum, leave these devices in the trunk of the car so that they will not be a distraction when you settle down for The Talk. This will also mean choosing a time when you will be able to forget about all your other personal and professional obligations. Block out as much time as you think you could possibly need, and then add a couple more hours. This will help your time with your son feel unpressured.

As far as your son's schedule is concerned, don't have The Talk close to a big event like final exams or the prom, anything that would tend to occupy his thoughts, whether he is concerned with preparations or simply anticipations.

Obviously, maintaining focus also means you shouldn't try to have The Talk while at an amusement park, in a restaurant, or during a movie (you'd be surprised at some of the stories I've heard). Venues that can't be completely private or totally free of interruptions are just not a good idea. You may have an amusing time, but you will not accomplish your goal.

Finally, whichever venue you choose, remember that The Talk must take priority over any secondary event. If you go fishing and the fishing area is closed, it doesn't matter. If you get lost on the way to the big game and miss the whole thing, so what! You may have wasted $150, but you still have your son away from his normal environment where you can have The Talk with him. It is The Talk we are after, not the event.

Create Anticipation

It has always encouraged my sons when I acknowledge they're becoming young men. So talk up The Talk. Let your son know that you are going to be making time for the two of you to discuss manhood.

A month or so before the event, let your son know in a general way that in four or five Saturdays you will be spending the day with him. As the time gets closer, give him some hints about where you two will be going and what you will be discussing. As the day approaches, give him at least one reminder a week. This helps assure that the time is not taken up by anything else, and lets him consider questions he might want to ask.

Set Clear Goals

Young men differ in their strengths, weaknesses, and level of maturity. One is apt to speak freely while another needs some help in opening up. With one boy, it may be best to go into great detail concerning sexual desires. With another, whether due to temperament or timing or some other factor, a less explicit presentation may be better. Each of the topics presented in this book should be discussed with your son, but each topic should be presented in a way, and at a point in his life, that serves him as an individual.

So what exactly are you going to talk about with your son? I have not provided word-for-word text, because The Talk you have with your son must be your own. This book does provide the key information you should convey to your son. Armed with this information, you will be able to deliver The Talk fully confident that you have not missed any important areas, and in a way that follows a good sequence of topics and maintains a good balance between topics.

As you make your preparations for The Talk, I suggest you plan to bring this book with you. Keep in mind also that The Talk is only the beginning of an ongoing process, not a one-time conversation. There is no way a single conversation can cover all the material to the necessary depth—at least, not without turning what is supposed to be a high point of your son's youth into a dreary, clinical exercise in sheer endurance.

Instructional Goals

Here is a good basic set of instructional goals for The Talk you have with your son. Again, with many boys a father will need to plan for an initial Talk when his son is age ten or eleven. Just to re-emphasize—knowing how much to say at this point is important. There is no purpose in telling a young man something before he is ready to hear it, and it might even prove unhelpful to him or to your relationship. If you think he is emotionally and physically mature enough to profit from specific information, tell him. If you think he isn't, then you should be completely comfortable leaving it out of the discussion and coming back to it in another six or eight months.

So, while you may not cover all these subjects in the first conversation, you should plan for all these elements to appear in your series of talks.

Don't feel tied to the order of the material as presented in this book. Every young man is different and no one knows your son better than you. Begin your talk where you think you and your son will be most comfortable, keeping in mind that a free-flowing conversation is as important as the material being presented.

Simply make yourself some notes or mark this book up in a way that works for you, and the process of using this book during The Talk should not be awkward. Here is the order of presenting The Talk that I have found to be most effective.

1. The practical gospel: Chapter 6
2. Physical development: Chapter 7
3. Manhood: Chapters 3 and 4 (chapter 12 may be more suitable for a follow-up conversation)
4. Sexual relations: Chapters 8 and 9 (chapters 11 and 14 may be more suitable for a follow up conversation)
5. Pornography and sexual perversions: Chapter 10
6. Work: Chapter 13
7. Choosing a wife: Chapter 14 (In many cases, this is best handled in the last of your official Talk getaways)

Relational Goals

As men we can easily become mission-focused and neglect the human element. Never forget that growing closer to your son is as important a goal as is the faithful transmission of information. Here are some excellent goals that can help revolutionize your father-son relationship forever:

- Changing relational gears to begin learning to treat your son as a young man instead of a child.
- Turning over the "unplowed soil" of your son's heart so that you might begin sowing truth into him on a regular basis.
- Expanding your friendship with your son.
- Becoming a trusted confidant.
- Setting the standard of always speaking openly and honestly about difficult or even hidden things.
- Don't expect him to see or accept the relational change initially. It may take time for him to see that you really are treating him like a young man instead of a child.

Determine now that you will be completely honest with your son, you really are setting the relational tone for the rest of your life. Your son has no one whom he can always trust for honest information about life's most difficult questions. Right now he probably trusts TV, movies, and his friends—not exactly the ideal sources for such critical life information. You have a unique opportunity to fill that void and become the kind of friend to your son that most dads can only dream of being.

Pay Attention

One of the most encouraging parts of Jesus' ministry was that he took the time to interact with those who sought him out. Jesus took time to listen to the centurion, the rich young ruler, the disciples, even the Pharisees.

Let me rephrase that so that we understand it more fully: God himself, the Creator of all, the Alpha and the Omega, the Almighty, the Lord of Lords, the King of Kings, took time to listen to the centurion, the rich young ruler, the disciples, even the Pharisees. Now that's amazing love and that is what you should show to your son as you lead him into manhood.

It's true that you are in authority, but we are called to be servant leaders like Jesus, not like the leaders of this world. Like Jesus, we need to take the time to listen, and in love direct or redirect our sons—just like Jesus.

This is the change I told you fathers about in the beginning of the book. You, dads, need to practice what you are preaching. You need to be growing in love and decidedly becoming more and more like Christ. What a great opportunity to show our sons what it means to grow in godliness right now, right in front of them.

As such, your conversations with your son on these subjects should be personal, encouraging, and uplifting. You must be prepared to change relational gears, shifting from command mode to friend-and-counselor mode as the moment requires. Do not allow this time to become one of lecturing or making demands. Instead, recognize from the outset that your son will be able to hear and receive some things and unable to hear and receive others—and that's all right. Regardless of his ability to receive any particular material, your communication must be filled with love for him, not judgment or criticism. He will experience your love when he sees your willingness to listen, your unfailing patience, and your continued encouragement. In your unconditional acceptance he will be better able to confide in you without fear of anger or reprisal.

The nineteenth century English novelist and poet, Dinah Craik, does well in summing up your son's need for Dad to be willing to handle his thoughts, ideas, and shortcomings with a gentle and honest hand.

> Oh, the comfort—the inexpressible comfort of feeling safe with a person—having neither to weigh thoughts nor measure words, but pouring them all right out, just as they are, chaff and grain together; certain that a faithful hand will take and sift them, keep what is worth keeping, and with a breath of kindness blow the rest away.[6]

As you plan and pray for The Talk with your son, you will be preparing to build the kind of relationship that will give your son the sense of freedom simply to pour out the "chaff and grain" together, as he trusts you to do the sifting with him. He needs this freedom more than he knows, and maybe more than you are aware. Take the steps needed to be that kind of father to your son. Both of you will reap a lifetime of benefits as a result of your faithfulness.

CHAPTER 5 REVIEW

1. In most cases The Talk should be initiated when your son is age ten or eleven.
2. When first initiating The Talk don't be surprised if your son's answers are not forthright. For most fathers this will

be the first time you have had such a frank discussion with your son.

3. Your goals for The Talk should include:

- Changing relational gears to begin learning to treat your son as a young man instead of a child.
- Turning over the "unplowed soil" of your son's heart so that you might begin sowing truth into him on a regular basis
- Expanding your friendship with your son
- Becoming a trusted confidant
- Setting the standard of always speaking openly and honestly about difficult or even hidden things
- Not expecting him to see or accept the relational change initially. It may take time for him to see that you really are treating him like a young man instead of a child.

4. Determine now that you will be completely honest with your son—you really are setting the relational tone for the rest of your life.

5. Remember, communicating with your son is about being available at the right times, not making the time when you're available.

PART 2

The Talk

Beginning "The Talk"

This chapter gets the process started. It emphasizes the attitude you need to bring to The Talk, tells you how to begin in ways that will encourage your son and set him at ease, and positions you to build The Talk on the foundation of the gospel.

Kerplunk

My youngest son, Andreas, is twelve years old and he loves to go fishing with me. We go out and spend an entire day on the lake just talking and competing for the biggest fish, the most fish, the best fish, even the best cast. Andreas is a true conversationalist—that is to say "the boy can talk some." After our day on the water we usually head to a local restaurant where we recap what we talked about all day—just the two of us.

On a recent fishing trip we were competing for the most fish and Andreas was winning. He had his favorite lure on the line and it didn't look like I was going to be able to catch up to him.

Then he got his line tangled up so badly that he had to cut his line. I always bring my wire cutters when we fish so we don't have to mess with a knife in the boat. Andreas took my wire cutters and snipped his line. "Kerplunk!" His favorite lure fell into the water and sank to the bottom. It took some time to convince Andreas that his best lure was not retrievable and that he had to choose a new one. Realizing that it was truly lost and that I was still fishing, he selected a new lure and snipped his line one more time to clean it up.

"Which lure did you choose?" I asked, wanting to see my competition. Andreas' eyes moved away from the line he was working on to get sight of his new lure and suddenly "kerplunk!," my wire cutters dropped into the drink.

Now there was a time when I would have become upset with his clumsiness, but I guess I've outgrown crying over spilt milk—finally. Andreas looked at me, and I at him and we both began to laugh. It really was funny and that laughter saved the day. My laughter at the situation actually created an afternoon that was more fun, more open, and more enjoyable. My son became more relaxed, without fear of Dad's wrath or reprimand or correction. We laughed at the situation the very moment it happened and in the laughter I reminded him to always work on this gear inside the gunnels of the boat. I didn't need to say anything else because the experience of losing two important items overboard had validated my rationale before I said it. I didn't preach, I didn't reprimand, I didn't tell him that he would have to repay me for the tool or the lure, it was simply the cost of having fun. Had I been my old self, worried about a few dollars, or bent on correcting my son's every error I not only would have ruined the day, but I may have soured my best fishing buddy forever!

Not everything is going to go well with the talk, so you might as well get over it right now, before you even start. If you're giving your son The Talk, it's a sure signal that it is time for you to change. That's right, you need to change! Change your attitude. Change your expectations. Change your mode of communication.

Change what you communicate, too. No one said this was going to be easy, but trust me, you'll be glad you did.

Check Your Attitude

From time to time, every father finds himself relating to his son on the basis of correction. Whether you actually speak these words or not, your son may hear, "You did this thing wrong. That other thing was pretty good, but could have been better." Or, "Why can't you be different in these areas?" It can be an easy habit to fall into. If that's true in your relationship with your son, even a little, then no matter how positively you have painted the picture of this time together, he may still be wondering if The Talk is going to turn into a marathon correction-fest.

That's why it is especially important that you enter into The Talk determined that this is not a time for anger, judgment, condescension, correction, or reprimand. Place your entire focus on encouraging, informing, and building a close relationship with your son. At various points in The Talk you will have to bring up areas where your son may be prone to feel guilty, or you may be prone to judging him. Determine right now that when you come to these subjects you will be very clear with your son. Tell him this is not about anything he may have done wrong (even if he has done things wrong). Reassure him that all men struggle with temptations of various kinds. Right at the outset might be a good time to share one of the struggles you have had to overcome and explain that a virtuous man is not perfect, but he is committed to becoming more and more godly. Keep at the forefront of your thinking that one important aspect of The Talk is to help your son understand how to deal with temptation like an imperfect yet virtuous man, not to feel bad about the struggle.

Checking your attitude may sound easy, but I assure you it's not. What if your son, right in the middle of your conversation, declares he's an atheist? How will you respond? What if he admits that he's been having sex, or dabbling in drugs, or any other of a

79

host of unexpected announcements? Or what if he seems unin-terested or put out that he has to sit through The Talk?

You will be tempted to become angry, to turn to immediate correction mode, or to reprimand him. Don't do it. Not now at least. Remember, it's not in him, or you for that matter, to overcome sin and temptation. It is in Christ though, and that's where you must draw him now more than ever.

It should be no surprise that your son is in some way sinning. I can tell you right now, without hesitation, that he is. The question is "what sins easily entangle him?" not "does he sin?"

Now, by taking the time to talk to your son about manhood, you have learned of an area that tempts him. Why? Because he felt comfortable enough to trust you. If you shut him down now, if you reprimand him now, you risk shutting that door of com-munication forever.

Be prepared to love your son unconditionally, allowing him a safe haven to bring his thoughts and sins to you.

Questions Are Good

At every point in the conversation, give him the liberty to ask questions. The Talk must be a two-way street. Your willingness to hear anything your son might want to say will help show him you are serious about this. If he is like most young men, he will be shy at first about speaking his mind. So, especially at the beginning, pepper your discussion with questions. Draw him out about his values, beliefs, and experiences (without judging!). It is important that he becomes a part of the conversation and not just an idle listener.

Focus on Joy

Throughout The Talk, you should continually hold out the beauty and rewards of a virtuous life. While we can never be virtuous in our own strength, the Bible is clear that "we can do all things through Christ." The Bible is equally clear in teaching us that true joy is found in following Christ, so when you come to topics that could easily turn the discussion in a negative direction—such as sexual temptation, sexually transmitted diseases, or birth control—keep your focus on the joy and freedom that comes with following God's plan for sex and marriage.

Do not dwell on the penalties and pain associated with poor decisions. Yes, you do need to acknowledge that sin can be attractive, and may even seem enjoyable at first (don't worry, your son already knows this!). You need to make clear that the path of rebellion against God and his ways always leads to a bleak and empty place, but do not allow yourself to slip into lecturing or emphasizing the negative. In fact, say as little as you can about the consequences of sin without ignoring them.

Get in the habit of always turning the conversation back to the positive, where the emphasis belongs. Make sure you say twice as much about the beauties of right living as you do about the pain and sin of wrong living. You want to draw your son toward a virtuous life, so keep the discussion upbeat and full of anticipation for the joys of a life well-lived.

Ready . . . Set . . . Go

With these things in place, you're ready to go. Many fathers find that getting started can be the most difficult part. What do you say? Where do you begin?

First of all, relax. You can't put your son at ease if you're not at ease yourself. This means being genuine. Resist any temptation you may have to try to relate to your son as a peer. (There is no way you can pass as an overgrown version of an eleven-year-old.) Your demeanor should convey excited anticipation with an underlying seriousness. Smile and joke around a little but always in a way that is natural for you.

So here we go. You're going to start by reassuring your son. You will do this by clarifying what your intentions are and are not. Here is a sketch of the information you need to convey from

81

the outset. Remember, it will be better if you can try to put these things into your own words. And when in doubt, keep it simple.

- You are coming into a new time in your life. You are beginning the journey from being a boy to becoming a man.
- Every boy walks through this process. Millions of guys have already done this. It's not always easy, but it's completely normal.
- There are outward physical changes that help us determine when the inward changes are due to occur: things like underarm hair, sweating, and sometimes acne or pimples. These are physical signs of maturity.
- You are not a man yet, but you have started the process. It is important as you travel this road that you have someone you can trust who will always speak honestly to you and will look out for your best interests. This needs to be someone who has walked that road and can give you the benefit of his experience. That is why I have brought you here, to talk to you about the things reserved for men to discuss.
- There are no questions that are off limits for this discussion.
- I will be completely honest with you.
- I will not hide anything from you that should be shared with a young man of your years.
- I will answer all your questions to the best of my ability.
- What we discuss here is a conversation between men and it must stay between us. You are not to discuss these things with any younger brothers. They are not ready for such discussions, and when they are I will discuss these things with them just as I am discussing them with you. Obviously, these discussions aren't for girls to hear, either, even though we will spend some time talking about girls.
- Many of the things you have heard and seen about girls and about being a man—things you think may be true and accurate—probably aren't. I want to tell you the truth about becoming a man, and what being a real man is all about. This

truth comes from Scripture, either through direct command or principle. The world cannot offer this divine perspective on sexuality.

Share the Gospel

Next, and this is critical for any Christian father, you want to review the gospel. Even if your son is definitely a Christian, you need to build The Talk on the fact that the gospel is the only source of forgiveness, provides the only true freedom from guilt and shame, and opens a channel of grace from God that meets our every need.

Sharing the gospel does not have to be long or complicated. The good news lends itself to a simple and pure presentation. All we are called to do is give our own testimony of God's life-changing grace. So, while you want to tell your son the basic facts of the gospel, you should also weave in your own experience of how the gospel has changed you.

You may want to use a brief, written version of your testimony, just so you don't miss anything. If you are experienced at presenting your testimony verbally, that's fine too. Just make sure you don't shortchange your son at this crucial time—present your personal testimony of God's grace clearly and succinctly. Your son needs to know that his father has direct, saving, life-changing experience with the amazing grace of God.

Don't worry if your testimony doesn't seem especially exciting or unique. It doesn't have to be. Pray for God to make your testimony powerful in your son's heart and mind. It is God who causes his truth to change people. It does not depend on the power of our words or the details of our own history.

As you discuss the gospel and your testimony, let your son ask questions. It's okay if you don't have all the answers. If necessary, say "I'm not sure about that," make a note of the question, and tell your son you'll get back to him (then make sure you do). This admission will not discredit your faith, your spiritual authority, or your trustworthiness in the eyes of your son. Believe me, he already knows you're imperfect! In fact, your real-life demonstration of humility will increase his respect for you. Then, once you have gone back to study and/or seek counsel on the questions you cannot answer, you will have a natural opportunity for resuming The Talk. Your humility and follow-through will be the first step in moving The Talk beyond a one-time event to a new lifelong conversation.

Here is a useful way to incorporate into your conversation the key elements of the gospel message (use some or all of the indicated verses to anchor these points in Scripture). Relax, as you are open and honest with your son about God's work in your life, God's Spirit will do the rest.

1. Man's nature is fallen and unacceptable to God. That's why we all need a Savior (Ecclesiastes 7:20, Romans 3:23).

2. Man is completely unable to reconcile himself to God. (Galatians 2:16, Ephesians 2:8–9)

3. God's love is shown through the saving grace of his Son, Jesus Christ (John 3:16, Romans 5:8, 1 Timothy 2:5–6).

4. There are eternal consequences for not believing in Jesus as God the Son, sent to become our Savior (2 Thessalonians 1:8–9, Revelation 20:12–15).

5. But simple faith in God's grace through the work and person of Jesus can and will save us (Romans 4:5).

6. This faith is the only thing needed for salvation—we don't have to do anything except believe, and there's nothing we could do that will ever save us apart from faith (Ephesians 2:8–9, Romans 5:1).

7. Simple faith is not an intellectual assent. It involves more than your mind. It must include a true trusting in the saving work of Jesus on your behalf (John 12:36, Acts 14:23, Romans 4:4–5).

8. You can respond to God's call to faith in Jesus by simply repenting of your sins in your heart before God (praying) and confessing your faith in the finished work of Jesus Christ,

God's own Son, who died on the cross to pay for your sins (Acts 2:37–39, Acts 3:19, Romans 10:9–11).

Not Too Bad, After All

As it turns out, starting The Talk isn't really that difficult. By the time you get to this point in The Talk you will have accomplished all these things.

- Started your discussion on an upbeat note
- Reminded your son why you're here
- Affirmed that you see him transforming into a young man
- Assured him this is not going to be about correction
- Laid out the ground rules for your discussion
- Shared the gospel with him

That's a great start! Now you're ready to move on to the teaching and discussion.

CHAPTER 6 QUESTIONS FOR GETTING STARTED

1. "As we get started, do you have any questions about this time, and why I have set it apart for you? I am hoping that this will be a fun and memorable time for us. It is a time of change for both of us. You are starting your journey to becoming a man, and I am starting to transition from treating you like a little kid to treating you more like a young man. This marks a time of change for both of us."
2. "Describe to me what you think a man is like. What does he look like? How does he act? What are the most important things about being a man?"
3. The gospel is the foundation of being a man. "Tell me, in your own words, what the gospel is? Why do you think the gospel is important to being a man?"

4. "Have you noticed any changes in yourself? The way you look? The things you think about? The things you like?"
5. "Does a man need to be perfect to be a true man? Explain that a virtuous man is not perfect, but he is committed to becoming more and more godly."

CHAPTER 7

Male and Female Anatomy

This chapter covers some basic information about the anatomy of men and women. As you move through these remaining chapters during The Talk, please keep in mind the material from chapters 5 and 6 about maintaining an encouraging attitude and a positive emphasis.

About Dating

My sons never really showed interest in girls until they were in high school. I think that was a real blessing from the Lord since I was able to have The Talk with them before they were really involved with girls in any significant way. It opened up an important channel of communication.

When my second son, Phillip, was seventeen he came to me to ask what I thought of him starting to officially "date" someone. I asked him some simple questions and as it turned out I already knew the girl he had in mind. I think he was really taken aback by my answer.

"I think you should start seeing girls," I said plainly. I reviewed with him how to guard his own heart and his girlfriend's purity. We walked through the difference between "dating" as the world understands it and "dating" that honors the Lord. I required of him that he speak with the young lady's father, and if her father approved then he would have my blessing as well. I was thankful that my son sought my counsel and recognized the significance of this decision.

You may or may not agree with young men and women dating at seventeen. Personally, I prefer my boys to go through that learning curve while they are still under my care and protection instead of being on their own in college somewhere else.

The decision isn't the point though. The fact that my son was "man" enough to come to me and inquire instead of simply beginning the process, is the point. It's difficult to believe, but he really is a young man now. It is time for him to start facing the world on his own, knowing that his dad is available when he needs a hand.

Anatomy of a Man

If your son has not yet begun to experience any obvious physical signs of maturing, he probably will soon. In any case, he knows they take place. His awareness of these changes gives you an easy starting point for a conversation on anatomy.

Keep in mind that these are not random changes, nor are they the result of evolutionary forces. These biological changes were planned by God. Your son can take comfort and have confidence that these things are part of God's plan.

If there have been any outward changes in your son, that's the obvious place to begin this part of The Talk. As you do so, remind him that:

- these are signs that a boy is beginning to mature

- the changes you are about to discuss with him are common to all boys, so there is nothing to be embarrassed about
- these changes appear at different times with different boys, and not always in the same order
- this means there is no way of maturing that is "more manly" or "less manly"
- he can expect to notice all these changes in the coming months and years

The Basics

These first four topics—body hair, body odor, growth spurts, and muscle development—don't need to be discussed at great length, but notice the opportunity you have here: Because these are not particularly embarrassing subjects for most young men, your son can get accustomed to the idea of discussing "man stuff" with you in a low-risk way. Your relaxed and casual style of leading the conversation will really help him here.

Under-Arm and Facial Hair: This is often one of the first and most obvious signs of physical maturation in a young man. If your son is not already shaving, would this be a good opportunity to encourage him to start?

Body Odor: This is another practical area of maturity that may need to be addressed. If your son is not already showering regularly, he should be as soon as body odor becomes at all evident.

Growth Spurts: Not much needs to be said about this area. Just mention that growth spurts may continue throughout his teen years.

Muscle Development: This will be obvious for some boys at a fairly early age, but not for all. Some men continue to develop muscle mass in stages, through their twenties or even their thirties.

As you cover each of these subjects briefly, casually, and naturally, it will set the tone for the next section.

Getting a Little More Personal

Here's where you start to delve into topics your son may find more embarrassing. As long as you stay relaxed, however, he probably will too. Just make sure you keep the door open for questions.

Pubic Hair: A lot of detail here isn't necessary. Giving your son the general idea about what to expect is probably enough.

Slang Terms: This may seem odd at first, but it will be helpful to your son if you make sure he is familiar with several of the popular or slang terms for the penis and testicles. Some of these terms are crude, unsuitable for mixed company, and inappropriate for a public context. They are not curse words, and in the way you will be using them they are not prohibited by the Bible's condemnation of crude or perverse speech. In this context they are just alternative names. They are also words your son needs to be aware of. So don't hesitate to say them—even if you doubt he will ever hear you say them again.

Circumcision: Explain what circumcision is. Recall Genesis 17, when God commanded that all the males among his followers be circumcised. Let him know that today this is no longer a requirement of the Lord. Tell him how circumcision is very often performed on male infants today for purposes of health and cleanliness, but that this is not universally done. Describe to him what each condition looks like and let him know that both are normal and acceptable.

Erections: Describe an erection. Make it very clear that erections are a perfectly healthy, normal part of maturity. Let him know that erections play a role in having sex and that you will be discussing this later in more detail. Unless you know the answer already, ask your son if he has had an erection yet. If he says no, you may want to press in a little further; embarrassment might be tempting him to avoid the question, hoping that the whole subject will just go away. If he is trying to avoid the question, be gracious and understanding.

Dual Purpose of the Penis: Here you begin to discuss what the penis is used for in sexual intercourse, but not how. (That conversation will come later.) Start by distinguishing between the urinary function of the penis and the reproductive function. Let your son know that while the penis is used for both, the two systems work independently—sperm and semen don't mix with urine. Go into as much detail as you think necessary, and make sure you define your terms well enough that your son understands essentially what you are talking about.

Orgasms: Describe an ejaculation, emphasizing that this is normal and primarily related to procreation (avoid any detailed discussion of sexual intercourse at this point). Then describe to your son sperm and semen, and in very basic terms the role they play in conception. Let him know that ejaculation is accompanied by a wonderful feeling known as an orgasm. Describe how an orgasm occurs in the detail you deem necessary.

Wet Dreams: A discussion of wet dreams can be tricky. On the one hand, Jeremiah 17:9 states that "The heart is deceitful above all things, and desperately sick; who can understand it?" If your son is dwelling on sinful thoughts and images during the day, they may very well influence his dreams at night. In this way, wet dreams can be a symptom of a sinful thought life. Frequent evidence of wet dreams indicate that it may be a good time to have a private discussion with your son about his maturation, lustful thoughts, and guarding his heart by keeping his eyes from sexual images.

On the other hand, wet dreams do occur naturally, and can seem quite random. While it is important to remember that "natural" does not necessarily mean "neutral," it is also important to remember that not all wet dreams are the result of lustful thoughts. This requires discernment and sensitivity on your part. You want to be clear when you discuss these things with your son, but you also do not want him to feel unnecessary guilt for something over which he feels he has no control.

In any case, your son will at some point experience a wet dream, and that should be expected. Help him understand that he need not be embarrassed should he have one, but that he should be able to discern whether or not it came from a lusting heart based on his thoughts when he wakes up—and remind him that if it did, the gospel offers him grace and forgiveness rather than embarrassment and shame. And on a practical level, let him know how he can discreetly handle such a situation in your household.

Masturbation: Describe how masturbation takes place (if he hasn't figured this out yet, he will soon). Let him know that resisting the urge to masturbate is a vitally important way to learn to control his sexual desires. When he was a baby, he had very little control over physical urges such as eating, sleeping, or going to the bathroom. He had to learn to control these physical urges as he matured. What a sad case he would be if he hadn't learned that control! Now he is in another phase of maturing and it is time to learn a new kind of self-control as a new urge develops.

You should also address the fact that all sexual sin is serious, with masturbation being no exception. Therefore, should your son choose to masturbate he will feel guilty about it, as he should. Indeed, it is not unusual for young men to have significant struggles with masturbation, and there may be times when he fails in his self-control. Yet Christ, who took the punishment for all your son's sins, even this one, is quick to forgive when your son repents.

While there is grace for a person who falls into masturbation and legitimately repents, the unrepentant heart could be setting a lifelong pattern that will follow him into adulthood—even into marriage. Your son needs to be strongly encouraged to understand that masturbating is a sin and that he can resist and overcome this temptation like all other temptations—through Christ who strengthens him.

As a matter of medical advice, your son should know that it is never a good idea to try to stop an ejaculation once it is underway by squeezing or otherwise seeking to stop the flow of semen. This could cause discomfort and physical harm. It is better to simply let the ejaculation run its course and then repent of the sin and praise God for his forgiving grace.

What Does a Real Man Look Like?

Now make special note of the fact that while every male will have the physical features just discussed, few boys will ever become men in the biblical sense of the word. Biblically, being a man has to do with humility, courage, purity, faithfulness, selflessness, and self-control, as we saw in chapter 4.

This is a vitally important part of The Talk. Your son must come away from these conversations understanding that being a real man is much more about character than it is about following a set of moral rules. Be prepared to stay on this subject for a good while; this is no time to skip over things quickly.

At this point in The Talk, review with your son the Six Key Virtues for Men discussed in chapter 4. I have repeated these key virtues along with their definitions for your convenience. Before you read each definition, ask your son to try to define the term. Encourage him to speak freely, but unless he has already been unusually well taught, his definitions will be way off the mark. That's okay. Commend him for even the smallest sliver of accuracy that may have been in his definitions, and then walk him through the definitions presented here, as well as the supporting Bible verses.

Humility

To pursue humility means choosing to accept the fact that your knowledge and abilities are limited, and in light of that, regularly seek help and graciously receive advice and correction.

Courage

To pursue courage means choosing to do what is right despite the opposition of others or of your own desires (often the more difficult enemy to fight).

Purity

To pursue moral purity means choosing to live by the highest moral principles in both speech and physical relations, despite your own desires to do otherwise, and despite any external pressure to compromise.

Faithfulness

To pursue faithfulness means acting in integrity, keeping your word, and doing what is right before God, with fortitude and without complaint, because you trust God to give you the ability to complete all he has given you to do.

Selflessness
To pursue selflessness means placing the well-being of others before your own needs and desires.

Self-control
To pursue self-control means maintaining full presence of mind in all situations and circumstances, and choosing to exercise restraint despite your desire or tendency to do otherwise.

Let your son know that the value of all of his actions rests on these virtues, and that it would be wise for him to memorize them and think about them often. Give him specific examples of choices that he is likely to be faced with, where the exercise of one or more of these virtues will be vitally important. He needs to see that, without these virtues, he will spend his life enslaved to selfish vices that will promise to fulfill him but will leave him dry, desperate, and alone. You might want to offer a helpful illustration from your life or that of a friend or relative, even—and maybe especially—if the story is sad or tragic (just don't exaggerate). You could also mention a sports hero or a prominent politician, depending on your son's areas of interest and awareness, who was derailed due to a lack of virtue.

Remind your son that no man is born virtuous, but that each man must choose whether he will act virtuously. It is up to him. No one else can make him virtuous, and the "force of gravity" from both the fallen world and his own sinful nature will always tend to drag him down, unless he fights. And fighting is about knowing the Word of God and calling out to God to change you, so that you can do more than sometimes act like a virtuous man—you can actually be a virtuous man. Your conversation may go something like this:

"Son, I want you to consider why so many 'great' men who appear to be virtuous fall into sin. Let's take Tiger Woods as an example. Tiger had every appearance of being virtuous. He was dedicated to his sport. He trained and practiced with intensity. He even set up a foundation that has helped thousands of children. And, of course, he was a winner.

"Still, there were signs of trouble. He had a quick temper. Bad shots were often followed by bad language. These, however, were only the tip of the iceberg. As the world found out, Tiger was anything but virtuous.

"That's how we all start out—enslaved to our sin, just like Tiger. We naturally shove aside the truth of God's word. We want nothing to do with virtue and purity, and no amount of discipline and hard work can overcome the powerful nature of our sinful flesh.

"Son, you and I were born with the same sinful nature as Tiger. I can assure you that you will struggle with the same things that destroyed his marriage. I know this from Scripture and from my own experience. I had to deal with these same things as a young man and I can assure you that no one is born virtuous, no one.

"What you need to understand is that no matter how hard you try, you cannot overcome these things in your own strength. That's what Tiger probably thought, 'If I'm just stronger, or more self-disciplined,' but it didn't work for Tiger and it won't work for you or me either. The difference between a man who looks virtuous and one who actually is virtuous is Jesus. It really is that simple.

"Son, this is the truth. Virtue comes only from Christ. You become a virtuous man, a "real man," as you trust in him. As we put God first in our decisions, in our desires, and in our lives, we begin to display the "fruit" of a virtuous life—the fruit of the Spirit of God, who lives in us. The aggressive pursuit of God is the only way to be set free from the lusts of our flesh.

"Our talk is about this pursuit. Son, Christ knows your thoughts and struggles. He was tempted with every type of sexual temptation that you will ever have. Yet he did not sin. Christ knows first hand what you will face. He loves you, not because you're perfect, but because he's your Savior. He proved his amazing love for you and me when he died to make sure we would be acceptable before God. This is really cool. It is through the power of his Spirit that you can be a man who bears the fruit of the Spirit.

"In Christ, you can be a virtuous man!"

Anatomy of a Woman

When you get to this subject, your son may be somewhat relieved that the attention is off him directly. In many cases, however, there will also be some embarrassment, because females—or at least some specific females—have probably begun to fascinate him in ways that nothing else ever has.

As you lead this discussion, be careful that the subject of the female body is not taken lightly or handled in a joking manner. All that you cover here will become the foundation for more difficult discussions later about sexual activity, pregnancy, and sexually trans-mitted diseases. So, while it is fine if the conversation is informal, do not allow it to become unserious. This is an opportunity for you to communicate to your son, by your words and your attitude, that a woman's body is a wonderful and sacred gift from God, intended for the enjoyment and admiration of one man, her husband. It is not something to joke about, ridicule, idolize, or regard as an object. Here your conversation may begin something like this:

"You know our goal is to become a 'true man.' We also know that we become a true man by pursuing God and allowing the fruit of his Spirit to dwell in us richly, but that's not always easy. How we think, talk, and interact with women is a perfect example.

"How God calls us to treat and think about women is in stark contrast to what we see in the media. It's not possible to believe or do both. As a man you have to choose to either believe Jesus or the views of the world. How you think about and treat women is one way to see plainly what you really believe. It's a more difficult decision than you might think. Many men are taken captive by the principles of this world by first compromising their views on women.

"On the one hand Jesus tells us to treat women with purity, kindness, and self-control. We are called to lay down our lives for them, to protect them and care for them in both word and actions.

"On the other hand the media and godless people tempt you to stray from the Lord. Think about the commercials, movies and maybe even conversations with your friends. They call to you saying that true men lust after women. Their goal is to prove their manhood by getting a girl into bed with them. Many times they want you to define manhood by the number of women you sleep with. They want you to believe that by putting yourself first, by stirring up and selfishly pursuing your own lust and desires you will produce the fruit of manhood. But scripture is clear that these false promises lead only to death.

> With persuasive words she led him astray; she seduced him with her smooth talk. All at once he followed her like an ox going to the slaughter, like a deer stepping into a noose till an arrow pierces his liver, like a bird darting into a snare, little knowing it will cost him his life.
>
> —Proverbs 7:21–23

"Pursuing your own lust and desires inevitably leads you away from Christ, where true manhood is found—in Christ alone. Proverbs 9 personifies the folly that bombards us every day from the television and the world at large:

> The woman Folly is loud; she is undisciplined and without knowledge. She sits at the door of her house, on a seat at the highest point of the city, calling out to those who pass by, who go straight on their way. "Let all who are simple come in here!" she says to those who lack judgment. "Stolen water is sweet; food eaten in secret is delicious!" But little do they know that the dead are there, that her guests are in the depths of the grave.
>
> —Proverbs 9:13–10:1

"Jesus is calling you as a man to battle against the desires of the flesh. He is requiring of you to choose a side. Just like the days of old when the warrior Joshua called upon each individual Israelite to 'choose for yourself this day whom you will serve,' so God calls you as a man to choose who you will serve.

"The truth is that how you choose to think about and treat women directly reflects your faith in God. You have the divine opportunity to explore one of God's greatest gifts to man through the loving, gracious relationship between a man and a woman. So many men miss this opportunity because they choose to believe the world's lie about manhood. They never experience the amazing wonder of a physical relationship that is overflowing with the fruit of a godly life—pure, holy, and spiritually alive.

"Will your talk be wholesome and edifying when you discuss women with your friends? Will you be committed to caring for and protecting the women that you know, especially a girl you are interested in? Will you reject the world's call to treat women as objects to be used and abused?

"When you make these types of decisions is when you decide to be a true man or not. You see, this discussion is about more than simply making a few simple decisions about girls. God has called you to battle. He has called you to manhood. As a man he has called you to choose which side you will serve.

"Are you able to answer his call?

"Let's keep in mind our call to purity, honor, and holiness as we discuss how girls become grown women."

Let's Talk about Women

Pubic Hair: As girls make their gradual journey to adulthood, their bodies undergo changes just like the bodies of boys do. Part of this involves the growth of hair in a young woman's genital area, as well as under her arms and to some extent on her legs. Girls usually do not grow hair on their face or chest.

Development of Breasts: Boys tend to get more muscular in the chest, while girls develop their mammary glands, also called their breasts. Each girl develops differently, but appropriately for how God made her. Some girls develop breasts that are large; others develop breasts that are smaller. This time of growth and change can be a very sensitive one for girls. Encourage your son to be especially wise and kind in how he treats girls during this time.

Rounding of Hips: Girls are also developing their figures at this time. Part of that process involves the rounding of their hips.

Women Produce Eggs: Just as boys begin to produce sperm for the purpose of having babies, girls begin to produce eggs for the same purpose. The eggs are produced in a woman's ovaries and are released down the fallopian tube and into the uterus to be fertilized by the sperm. (That's all you need to say at this point about how conception takes place.)

What's with a "period"?: When a girl reaches puberty her body begins producing eggs on what is usually a fairly regular cycle of about once a month. This process is accompanied by what we have come to call a woman's "period." This is the five to ten day time-frame (period of time) each month that eggs are sent down to the uterus. Eggs that are not fertilized are discharged from her body along with the blood that has been lining the uterus for the past few weeks. In order to be clean and sanitary, girls use any of a variety of feminine hygiene products (most commonly, tampons or sanitary napkins) to absorb the bloody discharge.

Orgasms: Girls, like boys, have orgasms during intercourse that are pleasant for them to experience.

Masturbation: Girls can also masturbate. Masturbation is no less sinful or unwise for girls than it is for boys. Girls need to exercise self-control in this area just as boys do.

Dealing with a Know-It-All

Sometimes when a father begins The Talk he finds that his son thinks he already knows everything about the subject. This may simply be a defense mechanism. The boy is trying to keep an uncomfortable conversation as brief as possible. Other boys, however, may honestly think they know it all, but unless a young man has formally studied the subject from a biblical perspective, this is extremely unlikely. Whatever the cause of the know-it-all attitude, this does not have to be a difficult time for you as a father. All you really have to do, in a kind way, is call your son's bluff.

When one of my sons took this position, he really thought he knew it all. He wasn't mean-spirited or resentful. He just honestly didn't see why any of this stuff about The Talk was necessary. For a couple of moments it looked like we might be at a standstill, but one simple request began to shift the dynamic.

Turning the discussion back on him, I said, "Okay, good. We'll start there. Tell me what you know about sex already. That way I won't have to repeat anything." (If you take this approach with your son, watch your own attitude. Your question needs to be sincere. He may actually have some accurate information, however, it will most likely be mixed with falsehoods.)

The way I posed the question forced my son into a position that was difficult and uncomfortable, but also very helpful. He could see that I was ready to be completely open and honest with him, that I was willing to take risks in the conversation and speak frankly. It turned out he wasn't quite so ready. His answer spoke volumes.

"You mean, just tell you how to do it? I can't do that . . . I mean, I could, but I don't want to!" Immediately some huge cracks developed in his know-it-all attitude, and his self-confidence began to crumble. As I gently pressed a little further it quickly became clear to both of us that his supposed knowledge base had serious gaps and errors. Then he was ready to listen and learn.

CHAPTER 7 ANATOMY QUESTIONS

1. "God has called you to battle. He has called you to manhood. As a man he has called you to honor him in your relations with women. Are you able to answer his call?"
2. "God gives us outward signs when a boy is beginning to become a man, things like body hair, body odor, growth spurts, and bigger muscles. Have you noticed any of these signs in your body yet?"
3. "Some more personal signs of development include pubic hair and erections; has your body started to develop in those ways?"
4. "What are the character traits of a real man? Why is character more important than looks or strength?"
5. "How would you define the following character traits of a true man—humility, courage, purity, faithfulness, selflessness, and self-control?"
6. "How do you become a true man?"

CHAPTER 8

How to Treat Women

In all likelihood, your son will one day get married. Do you want to know how he will treat his wife? In some significant ways, he will treat her no differently than he treats any other woman. His overall way of relating to women is formed during the time he is becoming a man. That's why this chapter and this part of The Talk could have a huge influence in the life of your son, your future daughter-in-law, and your grandchildren. You really are the patriarch of your descendants, as your son will be of his. For your son, and the generations that follow, the future has already begun to be formed. In this season of your son's young manhood, that future formation rests in your hands.

It would get awkward and unhelpful if, for the rest of this book, I was regularly saying, "Now tell your son this," and "Now tell your son that." So, just understand that even though in some places it seems like I'm writing to you, I am actually providing for your review and reference what you should be saying (in your own words) to your son.

A Misguided Oil Filter

I change the oil in my cars. I've done it since I was eighteen years old, so why would I stop doing it now? I figure I've saved over $2,000 over the years, enough to pay my insurance for a month . . . or so it seems!

I recently changed the oil in my son's car (he was on crutches at the time) and then I changed the oil in my own vehicle. I had three filters in the shed and all our cars use the same size oil filter, so I grabbed one and put it on his Toyota, then I grabbed another and put it on my Toyota. My twelve-year-old assisted so it was quick and easy.

My wife is a teacher and the next morning she took my car to work. I came out to the driveway minutes after she left to find a huge puddle of oil where my car had been sitting and a two-inch oil spill tracking down our driveway and into the street.

Immediately I called her on her cell phone to tell her to stop or the engine will be ruined. No answer. I called again and again. I was dialing frantically but to no avail.

Finally my phone rang and her ID showed up on my screen. "Did you get my message?" I asked relieved that she called. "No, did you call? The car stopped running and I had to coast to the side of the road. I don't know what's wrong but I need to get to school, can you come pick us up?"

I was furious! Why didn't she pick up when I called? Now the engine was "blown" for sure, and to make matters worse, my friend had just pulled in and we were going fishing for the day. Now all bets were off. I had to get my wife and kids to school, get the car towed to a shop, and probably start a search for a new vehicle. Why hadn't she just picked up the phone? Why do we have cell phones if not to get in touch with each other when there is an emergency?

My fishing buddy and I drove out to check out the damage and there was my wife, in good spirits and going with the flow. Being the knucklehead that I am I did everything possible to show my wife the error of her way.

"Why didn't you answer the phone?" I asked. "Now the car is certainly ruined, and I will have to junk it or replace the engine!"

"The kids and I were singing at the top of our lungs, so I never heard the phone ring," she replied innocently.

I was exasperated, our day of fishing was ruined, my car was ruined, my attitude was ruined—and it was all "her fault" for not hearing the cell phone ring.

We got her and the kids to school, and shortly thereafter the car was towed to a nearby garage. I gave my cell phone number to the garage to call me with the verdict when they got to my car and finally went fishing. All in all, it only took us two hours to get going.

A few hours later the garage called to give me the update. The news was worse than I ever could have imagined.

"Mr. Zollos," the mechanic began, "your car is ready for pick up."

"You mean it's running?" I asked in disbelief. "What was wrong with it?"

"Yes sir, it's running fine. Someone put the wrong oil filter on the vehicle, sir."

I wanted to say "Well, that's what I get for letting my wife change the oil!" but I was caught, tried, and convicted. This whole mess was my fault from beginning to end. I had blamed my wife and made her feel like she had done something wrong. I all but told her that she had ruined the car. I made a scene, I pouted like a little child. The way I had treated her was unfair. I was wrong from first to last.

I called my wife to explain the situation and I apologized for blaming her for my error. She was not as surprised as I was that the car was not ruined. "I've been praying all day about it," she said, "God is so good."

You know, she never scolded me. She never got even or made me feel badly about my lack of humility or how I treated her.

It's true that "God opposes the proud but gives grace to the humble" (James 4:6), and "The righteous shall live by faith"(Romans 1:17).

I learned more than a few important lessons that day from my wife. Through her the Lord showed me how unfairly I could treat my wife. I now saw clearly at least one area of pride and arrogance in my life. Her faith taught me a lesson in humility. My wife brought to the table the very things I was lacking.

We all need to be reminded of who we are and who we are not from time to time. It will serve your son to tell him your stories like this one so that he can begin to understand how and why he is to treat women with kindness and honor.

Walking my sons through the scriptural account of the creation of man and woman has been an effective tool for me. Pointing out what it means when God says that we were created, man and woman, in the image of God, has helped my sons to put their relationship with women in proper perspective.

In God's Image

To reset a foundation stone for this chapter, remember what we learned earlier about men and women both being made in God's image. In using the phrase "the image of God," the Bible speaks of a spiritual, not a physical similarity. Men and women have equal worth in the sight of God, for they are equally similar to him, with each gender designed to play a unique and equally important role in this world. The roles that God has established for men and women are different, and complement one another, yet before God they are of equal importance and value.

The Relentless Opposition

Despite this perfect equality of men and women before God, popular culture—remember the wheat and the weeds?—will not teach your son to treat females as equals who are worthy of respect and honor. In general, popular culture will teach your son to treat attractive women as objects of desire, and unattractive women as objects of scorn or indifference. Either way the message is that they are objects, not equals.

How will your son escape this influence? What will keep him from buying into these appeals to his innate selfishness? He must be taught truth from Scripture, and he must have models of a godly way to live. Active family involvement in a good church is vitally important and can provide some of this teaching and modeling, but your son will naturally look to you above all other examples and all other teachers. You can't opt out of that responsibility.

This part of The Talk, therefore, is about establishing a bulwark in your son's soul. The relentless waves of cultural deception will crash against him every day for the rest of his life. You must equip him to stand in the empowering grace of God.

Strength and Self-Control

In chapter 4, we saw that a key virtue of true manhood is self-control. This virtue is especially necessary for a young man to exercise in his interactions with girls and women. It is needed as a counterweight to his increasing strength.

As your son grows he will gain strength physically. He will gain new abilities, new desires, and a greater determination to carry out his own will. He will grow stronger in his mental and verbal capacities, in his social skills, and in his overall ability to interact effectively with the world. This is what it means for him to mature as a male. To mature as a man, however, means learning how to exercise these strengths with appropriate self-control. The more power a man wields—whether physical, mental, or political—the more he needs self-control.

Your son must see his growing strengths not as weapons to enforce his will, but as tools which, when properly used, will bring joy to his family, his work, and his wife. Encourage your son to continually pray for and seek to exercise self-control (allowing the Holy Spirit to lead him), especially when dealing with women. There are three principal areas in which this applies. These three areas are his thought life, his speech, and his physical interactions with women, especially as they pertain to sexuality.

Thought Life

From our thought life springs our actual life. It's true. When I was a young man I wanted to travel to Greece. I thought about it, considering what it would take to make such a trip possible and worthwhile. So I saved money, learned to speak some Greek, and made specific travel plans. What began as thought became reality.

When I'm at work I must consider how to solve a problem before I can attempt the solution. When I'm at home I should consider how to respond to a sensitive concern of my wife before actually responding. In fact, nearly everything we do springs from our thought life—whether recent thoughts still fresh in our minds, or past thoughts that helped form a particular habit or preference. What we think changes how we behave, for better or for worse.

It's the same for your son. Where he allows his mind to wander is of great importance. Yet he may have never once made a clear connection between his thoughts and his actions. One of my sons was convinced that what he saw on television or the internet would not affect him. This thought-action connection can be a very difficult concept for young men to grasp. Remember, at that age a young man tends to ridiculously overestimate his own abilities and to assume—without really thinking it through—that he controls the world and is nearly indestructible.

Scripture, however, depicts life as it really is. Therefore, it teaches us to pay close attention to our thought life.

Search me, O God, and know my heart; test me and know my anxious thoughts. See if there is any offensive way in me, and lead me in the way everlasting (Psalm 139:23–24).

For from within, out of men's hearts, come evil thoughts, sexual immorality, theft, murder, adultery, greed, malice, deceit, lewdness, envy, slander, arrogance and folly. (Mark 7:20–23)

The mind of sinful man is death, but the mind controlled by the Spirit is life and peace; the sinful mind is hostile to God. It does not submit to God's law, nor can it do so. Those controlled by the sinful nature cannot please God (Romans 8:5–8).

Set your minds on things above, not on earthly things (Colossians 3:2).

If your son is ready to hear this, let him know that learning to control his thought life now could have a profound impact on his marriage in another ten or twenty years. For example, I know of many families that have been deeply scarred by the influence of internet pornography on a husband. The husband's embarrassment at getting caught is the least of the problem. Far worse is the psychological trauma to his wife and the indirect effects on the children. And even if the husband's pornography consumption has not yet been exposed, he will inevitably bring to the bedroom completely unrealistic or even ungodly sexual expectations that can do serious damage to marital intimacy.

It all begins with thoughts and, quite often, failures of self-control in a man's youth. Sinful thoughts, acted upon, beget more sinful thoughts. Lust begets more lust. Thoughts that run unbridled through pornographic internet sites will eventually destroy the sexual joy and fulfillment God intends for marriage, stripping wives of their dignity and leaving families broken and divided.

When speaking to your son about his thought life, as with all the topics in The Talk, emphasize the good, positive aspects of maintaining a pure thought life and the godly fruit that will result. I like Philippians 4:8 because it presents this concept in the light of God's glory. "Whatever is true, whatever is noble, whatever is right, whatever is pure, whatever is lovely, whatever is admirable—if anything is excellent or praiseworthy—think about such things."

Speech

Encourage your son to make a lifelong practice of interacting with women in ways that are kind, uplifting, respectful, and completely devoid of sexual overtones. This includes how your son speaks to girls and about girls. It involves what he chooses to say, and how he says it. It also includes directing conversations with women so that they don't drift toward romantic or sexual topics. Chivalry—a much-neglected word that evokes images of armored men on white steeds—can simply mean treating a woman honorably. If your son chooses to be chivalrous toward women and girls, his speech will always be kind, uplifting, and respectful.

Daily Interactions

When it comes to daily personal interactions, inappropriate sexual overtones, whether intentional or not, can creep in quite easily. Body language, eye contact, and "friendly" touching can all cause problems. Signals can be misinterpreted, and hormones fight against the rational interpretation of one another's actions. You may not remember just how strange it was to wake up one day and find yourself drawn to women in ways you had never imagined. Urge your son to cultivate the kind of self-awareness and situational awareness that will help him exercise self-control in these areas. Tell him to live on the safe side of the line.

Teach him it is never appropriate to retaliate against a woman. Even when treated inappropriately by a woman, a true man does not fight back. If a woman whom he sees regularly gives him "the cold shoulder," he does not respond by ignoring her, being rude, or refusing to speak with her. He continues to be kind and civil. At the far end of the spectrum, a man must never strike a woman, even if she screams at you and slaps you across the face. This is not how an honorable man deals with a woman, ever.

At times, your son may simply need to avoid certain women because they pose a temptation to him in ways that are sexual, or romantic, or both. While this is quite different from ignoring a woman in a rude or spiteful way, it does not always look very different, so in practice it can be a difficult line to walk, especially in the early teen years when all of this is new.

As your son exercises self-control in his thought life, his speech, and his daily interactions with women, he will begin to build habits that will serve him and his family for the rest of their lives. There is still much to cover in The Talk regarding matters of sexual purity.

Passion and Purity

While a few men are genuinely called to celibacy, the vast majority will want to get married. Encourage your son that he probably will too. Tell him that part of the reason you are here having The Talk is so he can better understand what it means to be a husband who is faithful to his wife in all ways. Even if your son chooses to remain single, it will serve him well to understand the things you will tell him about marriage, sexual intimacy, and how a true man treats women.

Explain to your son that there is no greater earthly pleasure than the monogamous loving relationship between a husband and wife. Let him know there is nothing more pure, noble, or sacred than the man and woman who refrain from sexual relations before marriage, for faithfulness to his future spouse begins now.

The true man will choose to protect his wife-to-be even before he meets her. As this relationship is protected and preserved, it can one day be developed in fullness.

In Genesis 2:18, God observes that "it is not good for man to be alone." These are God's words, not Adam's, so in response God created woman as a suitable mate for man. It is only within the parameters of marriage that true passion, love overflowing, and complete sexual pleasure can be felt and expressed. It is the passion that says, "No other life will do, for she is truly the best part of me."

Until your son has a deep and abiding love for a girl, and has expressed his lifelong commitment through a marriage ceremony, he must not give in to the temptation to have sex with her or engage in any inappropriate physical contact. On this subject, God's Word could not be clearer.

> Flee from sexual immorality. All other sins a man commits are outside his body, but he who sins sexually sins against his own body. Do you not know that your body is a temple of the Holy Spirit, who is in you, whom you have received from God? You are not your own; you were bought at a price. Therefore honor God with your body.
>
> —1 Corinthians 6:18–20

109

It is God's will that you should be sanctified: that you should avoid sexual immorality; that each of you should learn to control his own body in a way that is holy and honorable, not in passionate lust like the heathen, who do not know God.

—1 Thessalonians 4:3–6

Of course, the message from Hollywood and most of popular culture is completely different. Casual sex is casually accepted by a huge percentage of the population. In popular entertainment, it seems that sexually aggressive women are everywhere, and that has had an effect on some women in society as well. So, while it is one thing for your son to exercise self-control in how he behaves toward women, temptation can move to a completely new level when a young man perceives, rightly or wrongly, that a woman actually wants to be sexually defiled.

This can be a difficult area to discuss with your son, but isn't that all the more reason that you need to have The Talk? If you don't address this area honestly with your son, who will? Sex at every opportunity can appear to be entirely wonderful, but as we will learn in subsequent chapters, the young man who abstains from premarital sex has protected himself and others from heartache, disease, pregnancy, depression, and emotional trauma—all of them common outcomes of sex before marriage.

Just take a look at the rich and privileged lives of our Hollywood stars, many of whom turn away from God to pursue their own desires. Hollywood is littered with the ruined lives of some of the "hottest" men and the most beautiful women in the world. You probably have someone that comes to mind even as you read this.

The tragic stories of broken relationships fill the tabloids and television gossip shows. One man is photographed with a mistress and another abuses his wife; and real-life battles are fought through lawyers and in the media. On any given day we are presented with dozens of marriages of "the rich and famous" that are falling apart.

But how can this be? These men have everything that the world says you need to be happy and fulfilled as a man. These men are handsome; they are rich; they have married one of the most beautiful and desirable women in the world; they even have notoriety. Isn't that enough to bring lasting happiness?

Obviously not. Don't be deceived. Despite their every appearance of "having it all," these are men who are unwittingly being led away from God and to their own destruction.

Hollywood stars, rock stars, and sports heroes have a huge influence on young men today. It is important that you reveal these cracks in the worldly armor so that your son is not deceived, and instead can experience the surpassing joy of a sexual relationship as designed by God.

Faithfulness Begins Now

Now is the time for your son to choose his path. Will he be sexually pure or defiled? Will he put himself and his future family at risk, or will he be a virtuous man? Explain to your son that it is foolishness to think he can make this decision when temptation is staring him in the face. He has to set his mind and will on obeying God before the moment heats up. If your son is to succeed, if he is to overcome, he must decide when all is calm, not after temptations are upon him. Let your son know that you believe that, by God's grace, he has the ability to be faithful, and that you look forward to walking him through this time in his life.

Now, let's talk about what exactly sex is.

CHAPTER 8 QUESTIONS CONCERNING WOMEN

1. "What do you think the Lord says about how he created men and women?" "Did you know that both are created in God's own image?" "What does that tell you about how God expects you to treat women?"

111

2. "Why do you think self-control is so important as you get physically stronger as a man?" "How does this relate to taking care of women?"

3. "Do you believe that what you allow yourself to think about helps to determine your actions?" "Why is this important for men to understand?"

4. "What character traits should be evident when we speak with or about girls?" "Is this the case most of the time or all of the time?"

5. "Why did God create marriage?" "What does that mean to you now even though you are not ready to get married?"

6. "How will you have the strength to treat women honorably in a culture that treats them like objects?"

CHAPTER 9

Sex

The Michelin Man

Each of my sons is very different from his brothers. For one, basketball opens doors of communication; for another, music. For one of my sons, hunting has brought us together as father and son like nothing else. If our hunt is successful, the teamwork and camaraderie that is built between us is unforgettable. If, on the other hand, our hunt is unsuccessful, the character that is built into my son is of great value. Either way, it produces a memory that we will both cherish for the rest of our lives, and the time I have had to look into my son's heart is priceless.

These riches, which are almost always overlooked by hunting antagonists, are worth their weight in gold, and they come in sometimes the most unexpected ways. It isn't the harvesting of game that brings the significance of the time together, it is the sheer time and relating to each other as men that makes the difference. It is having a memory that you can remember together and talk about for the rest of your life. It is an adventure that will never be duplicated and that will grow in importance as the years go by.

I had taken my son, then nine years old, duck hunting a number of times. I had only taken him to areas that I was familiar with and knew well. Our blinds could always be accessed by boat or over land and I had never needed to get my boy waders, since I could be relied on to meet his wading needs. One Wednesday evening, a friend called to invite us on a three-day hunt to a location where I had never been. My son and I were excited about going and prepared our gear for the early trip the following morning.

Upon arrival the next morning at 4:00 a.m. we were given a blind by draw and the three of us drove to the access point. After assessing the situation I realized that I had not fully prepared for this hunting expedition. This was a low marsh that we would need to wade through on foot in order to reach our blind. It was inaccessible by boat or by dry land and my son had no waders.

So what is a father to do at 4:00 a.m, with a memory at hand? The only thing a father could do in such a situation. My friend carried the guns and the decoys, and I put my son on my back (with the food, shells and other gear in his backpack) and began the long journey to the blind. I didn't realize just how far away this blind was, or how heavy a nine-year-old boy can be, until we were half way in. The blind we had drawn was the one deepest in the marsh, a journey of more than a mile. It was like walking through sand with a 150-pound sack on your back. The only thing more difficult than that trip to the blind was the trip out after a full day of hunting! As you might well imagine, I was tired and sore by the end of the day.

I was determined to have waders for my son by the following morning when we went out to hunt again. The area we were in was a bit secluded, but I decided to make the long trip to a not-so-local Wal-Mart despite my fatigue. To my dismay they had no waders that would fit my son! Now what's a father to do? Even a father has his limitations and I had reached mine! A new day's hunt fast approaching and still no waders. Perhaps my friend could carry him this time? No, I couldn't do that to a friend.

All the stores were closed by now and there was only one hope—Mom. I phoned home and sure enough, my wife came up with the idea. Drawing from her childhood memories in upstate New York, when makeshift galoshes were made by slipping a plastic baggie over socks, she suggested trash bags and duct tape. Why not wrap him in plastic bags secured with duct tape? He could wear his tennis shoes in and then change into his boots when he got to the blind. Brilliant! I felt a little embarrassed not having come up with this creative use for duct tape myself.

At 4:00 a.m. the next morning I found myself wrapping my son in trash bags and securing them tightly around his legs using duct tape. The bags puffed out with air in between the wraps of tape and he really looked like a miniature Michelin Man. We laughed and joked about "The Michelin Man" for a good fifteen minutes. We laughed at how fat he looked. We wondered if he would float if he fell over. We doubled over and wished that we had packed a camera. After our hardy laugh I slipped on his shoes and he waded all the way out to the blind without incident! What a relief! What fun! What a memory!

All these years later we can't for the life of us remember what we shot and what we missed, but we remember the Michelin Man vividly and we tell that story for friends and family every year when duck season rolls around. As for me, I will treasure that outing all the days of my life. I will never forget my Michelin Man, or the time we had finding waders, or that incredible "ride" out to the blind. It was a difficult, hopeless, and absolutely wonderful time with my son. That time with him opened doors in our hearts that we didn't even know existed.

Your discussion concerning sex can seem difficult and hopeless too. For me, getting started was the most awkward part of The Talk. Let me encourage you. If you are able to gracefully traverse this territory, you will most certainly open at least one door of communication that was unopened before. Take your time. Laugh about missteps. If appropriate, tell him your story about your first "girlfriend" or someone else's. Oh, and one more bit of advice—assume nothing.

Assume Nothing

Don't assume your son knows anything about sex, because whatever he might know is almost certainly off in some way. Start at square one by telling him, or confirming that he understands, that "sex" is short for "sexual relations."

Immediately affirm that God designed men and women for reproduction and pleasure—that sex is intended to be a good thing (as we discussed in chapter 3). According to the design of God, a man and a woman are granted the physical pleasure of sexual relations only within the boundaries of the permanent covenant relationship of marriage.

Your son has probably already figured out that having sex with a woman feels good. Tell him anyway. Tell him that sex is the ultimate physical pleasure between a man and his wife. Biblically, however, sex is far more than a physical activity. Sex is primarily a spiritual activity. One reason physical changes occur within the bodies of young men is so that they can bring honor to God through a biblical expression of sexual activity.

Isolating the physical act of having sex from the spiritual aspect of worship is simply the world's cheapened expression of God's intention—that sex should be a spiritual act of worship that brings with it physical pleasure that uniquely expresses a man's love for his wife.

The world says that sex is about self-expression, in effect, self-worship, but your son must understand that when we engage in sex it is first and foremost an act of worship. We are either worshiping God or something else; but it is still worship.

In God's eyes, avoiding intercourse is not the same as avoiding sex. This is an important clarification for your son to understand. Sex in the broadest sense begins with the heart. Therefore, any physical contact that leads to lustful thoughts in the heart is sexual contact. This physical contact leads to lustful thoughts which in turn leads to escalating physical arousal which may, or may not, lead to intercourse.

116

Explain to your son that sex begins in the heart and escalates to physical contact that causes arousal or increased sexual desire. This is a very important point because we live in a society that often redefines words to avoid the stigma associated with inappropriate behavior. (Dads, in case you weren't aware—and I'm not suggesting you tell your son this right now—a large proportion of young people today do not consider oral sex to be "having sex" because it does not involve genital to genital contact.)

It should be no surprise that the biblical definition of sex differs significantly from the world's definition, but this may be a point that your son struggles with. After all, sex as a spiritual act of worship is an alien thought to this world. As with the rest of The Talk, simply tell him the truth plainly and give him time to consider the things you are telling him, trusting that the Lord will be faithful to reveal the truth of these matters to his heart.

"Having Sex" Does Not Equal "Making Love"

Despite popular opinion, these two phrases don't mean the same thing. Making love is much more exclusive, wonderful, and fulfilling than simply having sex. Sex by the world's definition may be fun for a time, but it's exceedingly shallow. Making love requires a deep-rooted affection that originates in the heart. A husband makes love to his wife when he expresses his love through the physical act of having sex with her.

People do "make love" by having sex, but they cannot make love until they share a deep and abiding love for one another that exists apart from their sexual attraction. That abiding love is expressed through the lifelong commitment of marriage. Making love within marriage is an expression, through the most intimate of physical means, of a love and commitment that is already present and has been publicly demonstrated and declared.

The great lie about "having sex" prior to marriage is that it will improve or solidify a young man's relationship with his girlfriend. Let's be clear about this; sex outside of marriage will only work to weaken and destroy your relationship. There is no question about it.

Think about it for a moment. Consider what it means to be truly in love with a girl. I mean a deep abiding love that makes you want to spend the rest of your life with her. What comes to mind when you think of having this type of relationship? Really ponder this for a moment before going on.

Most men begin by describing a strong personal relationship with someone they enjoy being with; someone they can dream and laugh with; someone they desire to walk hand-in-hand with through life. Is it surprising to you that sex doesn't usually come into that picture until these other, more important things are in place?

Love is born from the heart, not from the sex drive. God's framework of marriage before sex helps us to keep our priorities right. As usual, when we glorify God with our lives it works to our own good. We serve a truly wonderful God.

God Wants You to Have Sex

It might sound strange, but God wants husbands and wives to have sex. He made us male and female so that we would enter into marriage and "be fruitful and multiply" (Genesis 1:28) by having sex and bearing children.

In his mercy, God has given us a plan, called marriage, so that our sexual relations might remain the blessing of joy and satisfaction he intended. Outside of marriage, however, sex becomes the single most hurtful and destructive force in a relationship. And nothing damages a current or future marriage like sex outside of marriage. To sway from God's plan—one man and one woman, for life—is to place yourself and others in great peril. Here you will experience shame, frustration, anger, and bitterness. This is not theory or over-simplification. It is the truth. Sex outside of God's plan will taste sweet at first, but without exception will be shameful, hurtful, and bitter in the end.

That's why you need to teach your son that he cannot trust his emotions. As he becomes attracted to a woman his emotions will rise up and he will be tempted to cast aside the truth of God's word to follow his physical inclinations.

That's the risk, and it's very real. The most important thing to know and to emphasize to your son about God's plan for sex is that following that plan truly is the path of joy, encouragement, honesty, and faithfulness.

God's Plan for Men

God's plan for us as men is to have us care for women in general: protecting and uplifting them at every turn. God has ordained that sex be kept within the confines of one man with one woman, in a lifelong commitment. This is what marriage is. Any sexual relationship that happens outside of this simple structure is sinful, and off the God-given plan for your life, your joy, and your happiness.

This plan that God has for us is wonderfully simple and full of wisdom. When God's perfect plan for men and women is followed, there is no worry about sexually transmitted diseases. There is no need for lying or deception. There is no chance of premarital pregnancy. There is no chance of embittering girls through sexual escapades. There is only respect, honor, courage, honesty, humility, purity, and selflessness, resulting in an abiding love that can be found in no other way. In the end, husband and wife are deeply blessed, and God is glorified.

As a young man honors God in all things, God desires to bless that young man (apart from the gift of celibacy) with a great wife and wonderful children in a truly loving relationship. A godly wife really is an amazing, marvelous help. And a godly marriage is a living testimony to God's grace, goodness, and wisdom.

No, it's not easy. Nothing ever worth having really is, but the reward is so much greater than the price as to be beyond comparison.

How to "Do It"

How much does your son truly understand about "how to do it"? You won't know until you walk him through the explanation, step by step (with less detail for younger sons), while watching him for clues as to what he actually knows. When in doubt, always choose to reinforce the truth. It won't hurt to review what he already knows.

Start by reminding him of anatomy and erections. Then remind him of the female reproduction process. Explain how a man and woman come together, penis to vagina. Throughout the conversation, emphasize the need for a man to be gentle and caring in the process. If appropriate, describe how sexual intercourse takes place in some detail, including how to please a woman. Then describe how the sperm fertilizes the woman's egg. From there a baby develops in the womb and nine months later the child is born.

Use your discretion here, but this may be a good time to describe foreplay, kissing, "petting," intercourse, and oral sex. That's right, even oral sex. The fact is that if he doesn't already know about it he will soon, and it is best if this lesson comes from you.

What's Love Got to Do with It?

Explain to your son that 1 Corinthians 13:4–8 is a good guide to understanding God's plan for sexual relations, in this case, especially as it applies to how a man should behave toward a young lady in whom he is romantically interested.

> "Love is patient, love is kind. It does not envy, it does not boast, it is not proud. It is not rude, it is not self-seeking, it is not easily angered, it keeps no record of wrongs. Love does not delight in evil but rejoices with the truth. It always protects, always trusts, always hopes, always perseveres. Love never fails."

When an unmarried man is walking according to God's plan, he will see the fruit of God's love working in any kind of dating or courtship relationship. Because he is seeking to obey God in that relationship, he will focus on developing it without having sexual relations. In doing so, he will be protecting the young lady's reputation by keeping her from shame and the risk of pregnancy. He will be patient, curbing his own desires in order to put God's plan first in his life. He will be kind and selfless by purposing to wait for the commitment of marriage.

Does this sound familiar? He will be choosing to be a virtuous man.

What's "Going Too Far"?

If this strikes you as an old-fashioned question, ask yourself, "why?" Has sex changed? Has God's plan changed? No. People have changed. The secular definition of right and wrong has changed.

The truth is that the sex drive is extremely difficult to control. What's the best way to keep a fire from spreading? Don't start one. What's the best way to keep a stick of dynamite from going off? Don't light the fuse. When it comes to anything remotely sexual, especially among young people who have little experience with sexual self-control, one thing will always tend to lead to another thing—maybe right away, or maybe the next time the two people meet.

Because of the risks of sexual temptation, many young men are choosing not even to kiss a woman until there is a decision to pursue marriage. Some have even held off kissing until the wedding. Scripture calls us to absolute sexual purity. As Paul wrote to the young man Timothy, "Let no one despise you for your youth, but set an example for the believers in speech, in life, in love, in faith and in purity . . . Encourage . . . . women as sisters, with absolute purity . . . . do not share in the sins of others. Keep yourself pure" (1 Timothy 4:12, 5:1–2, 22 ESV). There is no room for premarital sex in God's plan.

As with all of The Talk, what you decide to tell your son about "going too far" is ultimately up to you. Scripture, however, is clear: we are to be pure. Leading your son to believe that anything the least bit impure is somehow still okay is just not the truth. Again, you know very well that one thing leads to the next, and your son should know that to venture "around the bases" is not only inappropriate, but a difficult tide to turn back.

Growing a Relationship without Sex

Here's a claim we are all familiar with:

> It is impossible to build a strong and fully informed relationship
> with a girl without having premarital sex. After all, how do you
> know if your sexual relationship with your wife will be fulfilling
> if you don't test it out beforehand?

This argument, with its alluring appeal to the exploration of
"sexual compatibility," can sound logical, but it is absolutely and
completely wrong. A woman is not a car you take out for a test
drive. She is someone's daughter. She is a child of God, created
in his image. This idea of "testing the sexual waters" is nothing
but man-centered, self-centered compromise, and completely
opposite God's intention as revealed in Scripture.

If you are actually ready for marriage—which does not require
a test drive—you have come to the point of being able to say
the typical wedding vows: "for better or for worse, for richer
or for poorer, in sickness and in health, from this day forward."
More than that, without purity and a lifelong commitment, it is
impossible to develop a sustained, passionate, loving, and sexually fulfilling relationship.

What if your son has already been sexually impure in some
way? Is all hope lost? Absolutely not! If his heart can be brought
to a place of true repentance before God for disregarding his will,
and for defiling any girl he may have defrauded, then God will be
quick to forgive and to restore his hope for a future relationship
that is pure, wholesome, and satisfying. Ours is a God of love and
mercy. When we confess our sin and turn from it, he is eager to
forgive and wash us clean of all our unrighteousness. The death
and resurrection of Christ proves God's radical commitment to
the forgiveness of repented sin.

If you have identified a particular area of sin that your son
struggles with, now might be a good time to revisit it. What a
great opportunity to stand beside your son in faith and exalt God
for his great mercy and his loving-kindness shown to you and

your son. Thank God for the gift of the cross and then pray with your son, asking Jesus to forgive and restore him in relation to the sin he is dealing with.

It's about Promises More than Warnings

The truth is that even if there were no sexually transmitted diseases and even if pregnancy were not a possibility, I would still counsel my sons to avoid premarital sex. Why? Because the most powerful truth about sex involves God's promises to the faithful, not his warnings to the unfaithful, as real as those are.

God gives injunctions against sex outside of marriage for our good, that we might be blessed and benefit. As we obey God in this area we position ourselves for the joys of guiltless intimacy, abiding faithfulness, and a God-honoring reflection of the relationship between Christ and the Church. I know that my sons will find the greatest sexual pleasures within the boundaries of marriage, and I know that walking outside of those boundaries will undoubtedly end in strife, shame, or heartbreak. I simply want the best for my sons. Don't you want the best for yours?

Despite what your son might have heard about raging hormones and the power of his sex drive, God's grace is greater and more powerful. Because of that grace, waiting until marriage to have sex is completely within his control. He also needs to know that, despite the constant barrage of popular culture, not everyone is "doing it." There are many young men of integrity, thousands upon thousands of them, who are choosing to honor God, to honor the girls they know, and to honor their wife-to-be, by waiting until marriage to have sex.

Anyone can say "Yes" to the easy path of sin, but only young men of courage, integrity, and purity, empowered and convicted by the grace of God, can say "No" to the temptation of premarital sex. Even when your son is married, he will need mastery over sexual temptation or it can bring him and his household to ruin. Your son will make a choice—either to wait, or to have sex before marriage. If he makes the right choice, he will be on the path to mastery over his sinful sexual impulses. Help him make a commitment to that mastery now.

Out of the Blue

After having this part of the discussion with one of my sons, we sat for a few moments in silence. (Silence is good, so don't rush it.) I was just about to move on when out of the blue my son asked me, "Dad, what's oral sex?"

Now that's what I'm talking about! I could have spent hours with my son, fishing, hunting, bowling, camping, or at the movies without him ever feeling safe enough to ask such a personal question. I may not have thought he was ready for that subject, but apparently he did! When this kind of discussion happens you know you have created the open environment you were after. He was more than a little bit surprised at the definition and the complete answer I gave him. Most importantly, however, my son saw that I was truly being open and honest with him, as I sought to answer his every question in light of his age, experience, and knowledge. This is relationship-building in the truest sense of the word. It is a relationship that will pay lifelong dividends.

CHAPTER 9 QUESTIONS FOR DISCUSSING SEX

1. "What does God think about us having sex?" "Does he want us to be sexually active?"
2. "What is the difference between having sex and making love?"
3. "What role do the character traits of humility, courage, purity, faithfulness, selflessness, and self-control play in our decisions about having sex?"
4. "Why do you suppose godly men agree that the most satisfying and exciting sex is always practiced God's way?"

CHAPTER 10

Sexual Perversions

All Fall—He Rose

It's interesting how little time is spent in the pulpit working through the fact that there are so many people on the wide road that leads to destruction and so few on the narrow path that leads heavenward. It should sober us all, and perhaps if more of us understood the implications of this fact we would be more careful before calling ourselves Christians—many deceive themselves no doubt (see Matthew 7:22–23).

We all fall to temptation in some way, so it should come as no surprise to any dad to know for a fact that their son will also fall into one sin or another. In fact, of all the areas of temptation, I believe the area of sexual sin is one of the most prevalent for all men, not just teens.

One of my sons came to me one day to discuss a personal matter. He confided in me that he had been struggling in the area of masturbation and he wanted to overcome the temptation. I believe the Lord gave me wisdom in dealing with besetting sin that you may want to share with your son at some point. Here's what I told him:

"First, we all sin, so your temptation and fall should be of little surprise to anyone. It's impressive that you would come and confide in me to seek help and counsel. It shows that you really hate the sin and desire to honor God; so you are in a good place as far as that goes.

"As a young man I struggled with the same temptation until I realized that this was not a struggle against the act of masturbating. It's more about the place that the sinning is apt to take you—away from God. It works like this: You are tempted and you fall into sin, in this case you masturbate. Now what? You feel guilty, really rotten inside and you tell yourself you're going to stop doing that. Then, not ten minutes later you're at it again and you fall again.

"This time you pray and ask God to help you overcome, that you want to do his will and that you need strength for this battle. Not too long after praying that prayer you fall into the same desperate sin again. Now you begin to get depressed, and eventually start questioning God. You asked for help, why didn't he give it? You wallow in self-pity that is reflected in your lousy attitude.

"Does that sound familiar? Take a look at where you land after you fall. You are depressed, feeling guilty, and questioning God's love for you, or even the existence of God! That's exactly where the enemy, the Father of Lies, wants you to be—moving a little closer to that wide road. This is not the response of a child of God. A child of God rejoices in the truth.

" 'Rejoices in the truth?' you ask, 'You don't understand; I keep on sinning, and I can't stop!' "

"It's still true—when a Christian sins he can and should immediately rejoice in the truth—not the sin, but the truth. The truth is that Jesus died for your sin, all of your sin. He will not leave you because you falter. Therefore when you sin here is how a true believer should respond:

1. Repent of the sin, even if it is the third time in twenty-five minutes.
2. Thank God for the covering of this sin by his blood.
3. Praise and worship God out loud for his abounding grace and mercy.
4. Commit to reading a few verses of Scripture any time you falter.
5. Put your mind on things above on a practical level; that is to say be a blessing to someone.

"Do you see the difference? Even in sin the true Christian can and should rejoice. The discerning Christian will understand that "our struggle is not against flesh and blood, but against the rulers, against the authorities, against the powers of this dark world and against the spiritual forces of evil in the heavenly realms" (Ephesians 6:12).

"Now consider; if you were the one who was tempting me and your ultimate goal was to turn me from God. What would you do if every time you tempted me I ended up honoring God, praising God, and being filled with the light and truth of his Word? Would you continue that temptation? Of course not, because it's not having the desired effect. In fact, it's having the opposite effect—I'm actually being drawn closer to God!

"That's why honoring God in spite of our sinfulness works to turn the temptation away from us. It's not that we fall that matters, it's not even how many times we fall that counts. It's simply how we rise back up, trusting completely in the powerful work and mercy of Christ, and praising him all the more for it because of his ability and willingness to save us from it through Christ Jesus.

"Of course if you are not truly repentant, if you don't truly despise the sin, then you probably need to revisit the wide and narrow roads because the Spirit of God is not actively being felt in your life; and that reveals a much deeper problem than the 'sin of the day.' "

What Is a Sexual Perversion?

There are really two parts to this question. First, what is the definition of the word perversion? Second, what behaviors are sexual perversions? For the first part, the dictionary works fine. For the second part, we dare not trust the judgment of man. Rather, we must look to the Word of God.

According to *The American Heritage® Stedman's Medical Dictionary*, perversion is "A practice or act, especially one that is sexual in nature, considered abnormal or deviant." Synonyms for the word "perversion" include: "distortion, misrepresentation, contortion, untruth, corruption, misapplication, misuse, twisting, falsification," and "lie," as presented in the *Collins Essential Thesaurus 2nd Edition*. In short, a sexual perversion is a sexual act that is abnormal or deviant.

Deviant or abnormal from what? The world's definition of normal and abnormal, what is true and false, is constantly shifting. The unchanging Word of God is the only trustworthy standard of right and wrong. Scripturally, a man who is perverted is one who deviates from uprightness.

Heed the Lessons

Some people would like your son to believe there is no such thing as a sexual perversion. "To each their own" and "tolerance" are the battle cries of those who would promote this thinking, but Scripture will not allow us to accept that view, for Romans 1:18–29 is absolutely clear.

> [18]The wrath of God is being revealed from heaven against all the godlessness and wickedness of men who suppress the truth by their wickedness, since what may be known about God is plain to them, because God has made it plain to them. For since the creation of the world God's invisible qualities—his eternal power and divine nature—have been clearly seen, being understood from what has been made, so that men are without excuse.

²¹For although they knew God, they neither glorified him as God nor gave thanks to him, but their thinking became futile and their foolish hearts were darkened. Although they claimed to be wise, they became fools and exchanged the glory of the immortal God for images made to look like mortal man and birds and animals and reptiles.

²⁴Therefore God gave them over in the sinful desires of their hearts to sexual impurity for the degrading of their bodies with one another. They exchanged the truth of God for a lie, and worshiped and served created things rather than the Creator—who is forever praised. Amen.

²⁶Because of this, God gave them over to shameful lusts. Even their women exchanged natural relations for unnatural ones. In the same way the men also abandoned natural relations with women and were inflamed with lust for one another. Men committed indecent acts with other men, and received in themselves the due penalty for their perversion.

²⁸Furthermore, since they did not think it worthwhile to retain the knowledge of God, he gave them over to a depraved mind, to do what ought not to be done. They have become filled with every kind of wickedness, evil, greed and depravity. . . . they not only continue to do these very things but also approve of those who practice them.

—Romans 1:18–32

You may be so familiar with this passage that it seems to have lost some of its power. If you follow along with me, however, I think you will have something significant and convicting to tell your son.

This passage reveals that when people refuse to worship and honor God for who he is, they literally change both mentally and morally. Thinking becomes futile. Hearts become dark. Minds become depraved. Those who once acknowledged God become utter fools.

How does this change happen? Where does it come from? The answer is a surprising one. After a while, God lets them have what they insist on getting. We see from verse 24 that without the knowledge of God, men's hearts become full of sexually impure desires, and God lets them have what they insist on having.

Verses 26–28 tell us clearly that sexual perversions are "shameful lusts" that come from "depraved minds." We are all susceptible to being ensnared by them when we turn away from God.

Deceived in Their Sin

Like all sin, sexual perversion is neither given nor approved of by God. In fact, it is in blatant opposition to God's will.

Notice the key words used in Romans 1:29, "They have become filled with every kind of wickedness, evil, greed and depravity." We also see two key points:

- "Sexual impurity" is always negative in the sight of God
- Homosexuality, both male and female, is plainly named as one example of a shameful lust that is unnatural, indecent, and outside of God's plan for sexuality (vv. 26–27).

People who take God-given sexual joys and exchange them for the sinful desires of their own hearts are, by definition, sexual perverts. These individuals, when unrepentant, actively and willingly take part in perverted sexual relations. They do these things themselves and approve of others who practice them (v. 32). Rarely, however, will the pervert recognize and acknowledge that these acts are unnatural or perverted. In fact, they will construct elaborate explanations and philosophical arguments in their attempts to justify their perverted behaviors.

Common Perversions

Here are some of the most common sexual perversions. It's worth reminding your son that for something to be a sexual perversion it must be engaged in willfully, the victim who has suffered through molestation or rape, for example is neither guilty nor in sin.

Consuming Pornography

Pornography is the explicit depiction or exhibition of sexual activity in literature, films, photography, or some other medium. Consuming pornography qualifies as a perversion because the entire purpose of pornography is to inspire and endorse lust.

Sometimes a teen may think that looking at pornography isn't going to affect him. "I'll just put it down and leave it behind," he may reason. He needs to understand that it's not that simple. Pornographic images do not simply go away once you are done looking at them. They remain etched in your mind and remain in your memory for long periods of time. It takes God's power through prayer and repentance to remove that image from your memory, so looking at pornography cannot be taken lightly.

Lust

An intense or unrestrained sexual craving—whether or not it is acted upon—that encourages participation in, or the visualization or imagination of, sexual fantasies. A spouse thinking sexual thoughts about their husband or wife does not qualify as "lust" since they are within the boundaries of joy set by God. Lust will always involve a craving for some form of sexual perversion.

Premarital Sex

Sexual activity between people who are not married to each other. Also known as fornication.

Adultery

Sexual intercourse between a married person and anyone other than his or her spouse.

Orgies

Three or more people having sexual relations with one another at the same time.

Homosexuality
Sexual activity between people of the same gender.

Bisexuality
A sexual attraction to both males and females. Bisexuality is therefore a perversion that combines homosexual and heterosexual behavior.

Pedophilia
The sexual attraction of an adult to children.

The list does not end there. For our purposes, however, there is not much point in trying to name and define every perversion. As you seek throughout The Talk to instill in your son the centrality of marriage, and the importance of purity in his relationships, you will reinforce in him a clear understanding of what is natural so that he will be better able to discern what is unnatural.

A Virtuous Man Will Be Politically Incorrect

The world will undoubtedly continue trying to redefine legitimate sexuality to include an ever-increasing list of things that God calls perversions. This means God's people will be called to walk an ever more challenging path. Indeed, any conversation in the twenty-first century that pits a cultural view of sexuality against the biblically faithful view is going to be politically charged. As time goes on, opposition to a godly perspective can be expected to become more and more intense. Already, some professing Christians are claiming that Scripture endorses one perversion or another. Others are teaching that Scripture is no longer relevant to sexuality in this "age of social progress."

Moreover, perversions are quite often practiced by people who seem kind and gentle and speak fluently the language of political correctness—which today is seen as a sign of insight, wisdom, and sophistication. Therefore, it will be important in The Talk to help your son learn to engage the issue in a godly way. Echoing the virtues of manhood discussed in chapter 4, your son must know how to face perversion with courage, honesty, humility, purity, and selflessness.

Courage and Honesty in the Face of Perversion

Explain to your son that there is a difference between being tolerant and being accepting of a lifestyle. It is right to be tolerant of those who are lost and deceived by their own wicked hearts, but it is wrong to honor, accept, or validate a perverse lifestyle as normal or righteous.

To tolerate something, in the political sense, traditionally meant politely putting up with it, even if it differed from what is true and right. Today, however, tolerance has become synonymous with full acceptance and complete legitimacy. To be "tolerant" of premarital sex or homosexuality, for example, now means to consider them as perfectly acceptable and morally legitimate, as long as everyone involved is a consenting adult—but that is acceptance, not tolerance. There's a big difference.

Faced with this ongoing redefinition of truth, your son should seek God for the following things.

- courage to be willing to lovingly confront those who promote perverted lifestyles, and refuse to recognize such lifestyles as normal, decent, or acceptable
- discernment to know when and how to engage people in this way, always making a clear distinction between respecting the individuals yet rejecting the sin that has captured them
- boldness to stand up and defend any person (we are all made in the image of God) against physical or verbal assault, regardless of their "lifestyle"
- honesty to speak truth plainly and graciously
- conviction to accept the persecution that will surely come whenever he does these things, being prepared even to lose the friendship of those offended by his message of hope

To refuse to validate perversion, to refuse to stand silently by when perversion is portrayed as a morally valid alternative, is to be a beacon of God-glorifying righteousness in our society. Those seduced by the allurement of the sin of sexual perversion desperately need to hear God's message of truth and hope. With your help, your son can be one who points the way with courage, honesty, and love.

There is no question that whoever brings this message of hope and mercy will be confronted, ostracized, and ridiculed. Being part of a strong local church is imperative for wisdom, strength and support, especially when it comes to temptations and battles that are associated with perversions. Such a church will have leaders who have strong convictions about purity and perversions who can provide appropriate biblical teaching on right thinking. The church is also important in that it gives your son the opportunity to have friends who have the same beliefs, face similar battles, struggle with similar temptations, and are committed to reading and understanding the Word of God which is a means of grace and needs to be taken advantage of.

Humility in the Face of Perversion

If God's message of hope and truth is to take root in a heart trapped by sin, it must be delivered with humility. When your son has a clear understanding of the gospel, however, humility in this area should not be difficult.

God loves and wants to save lost sinners. Every Christian's testimony is one of being a lost sinner, saved by the love of God solely through the finished work of Christ Jesus. With this in mind, the sin of those ensnared in a perverted lifestyle is recognized as the same stuff of your own testimony. Humility before God will allow your son to understand and express the love that God has for sinners. It will protect him from casting judgment and equip him to present a message of truth, hope, and life.

Whenever a Christian speaks to unbelievers about sexuality, this truth needs to be clearly and humbly expressed. Ours is a mission of mercy, not intimidation, disrespect, hostility, superiority, or rejection. We must bring to these conversations the same loving-kindness our Father in heaven has shown us. Our goal should be to plainly address the sin of the perpetrator, and present God's offer to leave that lifestyle and instead follow the Lord. This is a kind and merciful service to those trapped in this bondage.

Our prayer is that those who participate in perversions will turn away from the life of sin that leads to death, and turn toward the gift of God that brings godliness, sanctification, and life. Out of love we should willingly risk persecution or ridicule so that even one person might hear the call of God and be saved from death and damnation. Indeed, your son should be ready to celebrate before the Lord for the power of the gospel going forward when he has lovingly confronted sinful behavior and shared the merciful, redeeming good news of the gospel.

Purity and Selflessness in the Face of Perversion

There is no doubt about it, your son's own heart will tempt him to perversion. Whether adultery, pornography, homosexuality, orgies, or any other vain imagination, he will encounter some or all of the temptations we have discussed here.

With Scripture so clear on the topic of perversion, it is essential that your son recognize the danger of taking part in any and all such activities. He is called to be pure even if he is invited to participate in an orgy, is sexually pursued by the most beautiful girl in school, or is "strangely attracted" to another male. Actively relying on God's grace for mercy and strength, he should remain self-controlled and resist all temptation to act on the sinful desires of his heart.

How will your son respond when he is tempted by perversion? The Talk is your opportunity to prepare him for some of the toughest tests a man can face.

CHAPTER 10 QUESTIONS FOR DISCUSSING PERVERSIONS

1. "What do you think it means to be perverted?" "How does the Bible explain perversion?"

135

2. "What is the difference between a sexual pervert's sin and your own sin?" There is no difference; the penalty for sin is death. The only difference between one sinner and the next is the saving work of Christ Jesus that allows us to see our sin and gives us an undying desire to turn from our sin and follow him.

3. "How do you think a true man will deal with those trapped in a perverted lifestyle?"

4. "Is it possible to actually care for the person who is trapped in his or her sin while explicitly standing against the sin itself?" "How do you think that works?"

5. "Which perversions are okay to participate in?"

PART 3

Continuing The Talk

CHAPTER 11

What Is Safe Sex?

This day I call heaven and earth as witnesses against you that I have set before you life and death, blessings and curses. Now choose life, so that you and your children may live and that you may love the LORD your God, listen to his voice, and hold fast to him. For the LORD is your life, and he will give you many years in the land he swore to give to your fathers, Abraham, Isaac and Jacob.

—Deuteronomy 30:19–20

This is the "Life or Death" chapter, outlining some of the worst consequences that can result from premarital sex. When it comes to Sexually Transmitted Diseases (STDs) it can literally come down to life or death. This may not be material you cover in detail in your first meeting with your son, but you should cover all or most of it eventually. When you do, remember that even if you spend a good while on the bad news of sexually transmitted diseases (STDs), and even if it does get a little scary for your son (which is okay: the fear of the Lord brings wisdom) make sure at the beginning and the end of the discussion that you emphasize not so much the threats of premarital sex, but the blessings of obeying God and following his plan.

You don't want your son to make his decisions about sexual relationships primarily out of fear, but out of a conviction about what is good and right. Help him focus more on the good stuff than on the bad stuff. That is, more on the joy, passion, and fulfillment of godly sexual pleasure within marriage, than on STDs or pregnancy, the subject of the next chapter. Help him dwell more on the value of the pure relationship and less on the implications of the impure. Put the emphasis on having the courage to do what is right, not on the fear of paying for doing what's wrong. Help him envision first of all the virtuous man he can become, and only second the compromised man he can avoid becoming.

A Common Misconception

When you're ready to introduce this topic, ask your son some questions to regain his attention.

- What do you think is the worst physical thing that can result from having sex outside of marriage?
- Do you know what a Sexually Transmitted Disease is?
- Can you name one?
- Do you know anybody who has one?

If he says he doesn't know anyone with an STD, explain to him that he probably does. It's just that teens who have them naturally want to hide it out of embarrassment. Then, if they continue to engage in sex, they may spread whatever diseases they have to someone else.

Let him know that most people think pregnancy is the top concern when it comes to teen sex. This was once true, but not anymore. A pregnancy outside of marriage is a deeply serious thing, but all men, and the vast majority of women, will live through an out-of-wedlock pregnancy and suffer little or no lasting physical harm. STDs are another matter. They can infect both men and women with painful, humiliating, often incurable afflictions, some of which can kill you. STDs are unquestionably the primary physical threat when it comes to premarital sex.

Some Basic Facts About STDs

There are two types of Sexually Transmitted Diseases: bacterial and viral.

- Bacterial STDs include Chlamydia, syphilis, gonorrhea, and others. If treated properly with antibiotics, they can usually be cured. However, bacterial STDs can be painful and embarrassing, and even when cured they rarely leave a person without some type of damage.
- Viral STDs include HIV/AIDS, genital warts, some forms of herpes, and others. Viral STDs cannot be cured. Some treatments can reduce symptoms or slow the progression of certain diseases, but viral STDs stay with you for life.

  Some STDs, like Chlamydia, have no symptoms. If left untreated, however, they can lead to other serious diseases and conditions.

  In the United States the statistics on STDs are nothing short of alarming.
- In 1950 there were five known STDs, all of which are bacterial infections and therefore treatable with antibiotics.
- In 2009 there were more than thirty known STDs, 15 percent of which are viral infections and therefore incurable, as explained above. If you get a viral STD you will live with it for the rest of your life.
- Sexually active girls who take a contraceptive drug (the pill, patch, etc.) are ten times more likely to contract an STD than those who are not on a contraceptive drug.
- Within the next 24 hours 14,000 teenagers will be infected with an STD.
- On average, a teen girl who is pregnant carries 2.3 STDs.

141

- Almost half of sexually active singles, 47 percent, have genital herpes. This form of herpes is so common that TV commercials advertise prescription medications to help people live with it.

- Chlamydia is more common among teens than among older people. It has no symptoms and over time can result in permanent sterilization in women.

- One in four females, 25 percent, age fifteen to ninteen have HPV (Human Papilloma Virus). HPV can cause genital warts, but you can have HPV without the warts. Some forms of HPV lead to cancer, and these forms are the leading cause of cervical cancer in women, killing more women than HIV/AIDS.[2]

How to Have Safe Sex

The only really accurate definition of "safe sex" is having sex with only one person, who has never had sex with anyone else, in a monogamous and lifelong relationship. Everything else is just an exercise in damage control. Every other approach is simply an attempt to lower the risk, because the risk can never be eliminated. Condoms do not remove the risk. Techniques do not remove the risk. Creams and devices do not remove the risk.

Only one thing removes the risk—when two people get married and each one has sex for the first time on their wedding night. In fact, the odds are pretty good that if you have premarital sex or extra-marital sex you will contract an STD.

Here's a scenario you might want to describe to your son, using your own words and changing the details as you think best.

Suppose you "only did it once" and it was "almost on accident," but you contract a viral STD. Then, five years later you meet the girl of your dreams. She is made for you. She's the most beautiful woman you can imagine. You love the way she thinks, the way she laughs, the way she moves, and she is really in love with you. All you can think about is how you are going to ask her to marry you and the joy you will have together for the rest

142

of your lives! Finally you work up the nerve and, on one knee, you pop the question. It will probably go something like this:

"I love you so much. I find myself wanting to be with you all the time. I think about you constantly, your beauty; your laugh; how you are kind to everyone you meet. I would trade the whole world to spend a single day in your presence. Would you please marry me, I love you so much. Please say 'Yes' so I can spend the rest of my life with you. Oh, and by the way, I have an incurable Sexually Transmitted Disease. I take medication that helps with the symptoms, but if we get married you'll get it too. Then both of us will have it for the rest of our lives. Now, would you marry me?"

That's probably not quite the way your son imagines popping the question. You could also turn the example around, what if your son has been faithful but the girl he loves turns out to have an STD? This turn-about can lead to some deep considerations and insightful conversation with your son.

Thinking Right

Tell your son that the diligence and self-control that come from trusting God are necessary to remain pure. Let him feel encouraged and empowered by God's grace to be the man he was created to be. Look at all the pain and heartache and complications he's avoiding by obeying Scripture. God's promises are so much better than the ways of the world![3]

Birth Control

In addition to STDs, the other major area having to do with sex is birth control. Why does your son need to know about this? After all, your hope and prayer is that he will never have occasion to use birth control before he is married. So, why include this material in The Talk?

One reason is to demystify the subject and give him the facts, so he does not receive a false education from questionable sources.

143

Another is that in all likelihood he will need to know about birth control someday, because nearly all husbands and wives use some form of birth control for some portion of their marriage. Third, in our society, learning about the various methods of birth control is simply part of coming into manhood and understanding something about sexuality. Finally, covering this subject fits naturally into the rest of your conversation, and you are the best person to teach him these things.

The Truth about Birth Control and Your Son

The chart in Appendix B covers the most common methods of birth control in use today. Under ideal circumstances, each of these methods provides significant protection against pregnancy, compared to using no birth control at all. A quick reading of the chart reveals "effectiveness rates" of 90 percent or higher. This is one of the basic medical facts of birth control, but 1) that fact needs a little interpreting, and 2) it is not the only medical fact.

- Effectiveness rates are ideal numbers that assume contraceptives are used perfectly. That is, most forms of birth control require the woman and/or the man to take some action, in a specific way and at a specific time, in order for the method to work as intended. Make a mistake, and the effort can become far less effective, if not outright useless. Teens are not known for their ability to either plan or follow through. Consider the simple things they are already called to do: homework, making their bed, keeping their room clean. Would you say your son does those things perfectly? If he is sexually active, the odds are pretty good that in the heat of the moment he, his partner, or both will throw caution to the wind and be less than careful in the application of their birth control method.
- Even when used perfectly, no form of birth control is essentially 100 percent effective (except for abortion and sterilization).

144

- While some birth control methods (when rightly used) offer some protection against STDs, they provide no protection from some of the worst STDs.

- So, while numbers above 90 percent for preventing conception can seem impressive, the reality is that if your son is sexually active he will likely face one or more of the negative consequences associated with pregnancy or STDs.

In addition, teen boys have no legal authority over the decisions their pregnant partner may make in relation to a pregnancy. Should your son become a father before marriage, he could be responsible for $60,000 to $80,000 in child support payments over the following sixteen years, even if he has to go into serious debt to make those payments.

How to Communicate That Truth

When a form of birth control fails, it fails completely. No matter how "effective" that form of birth control promised to be, when it fails, the result is exactly the same as if no birth control at all were used: A child is conceived. As I said earlier in this chapter, there is no safe sex outside of marriage. The premarital birth-control game is like playing Russian Roulette with both STDs and untimely pregnancies.

Your son needs to understand this. At the same time, however, I do not suggest you make this the center of your emphasis.

Instead, like every other portion of The Talk, let your conversation be grounded in the spiritual and moral truths drawn from Scripture: God tells us to avoid premarital sex for our good and his glory, for these things are sinful and indulging in them will only harm ourselves and others. When an unmarried young man has sex he is disobeying God and disobeying his parents. He is morally defrauding himself, his future spouse, the girl he has sex with, and her future spouse.

The moral argument is not only the best reason for avoiding premarital sex. It can remain persuasive when the medical argument seems to fail. For at some point, in a time of weakened spirituality and increased worldly influence, your son will almost certainly take another look at birth control "effectiveness rates" above 90 percent and let his mind wander toward premarital sex.

Bolstered by that sense of invincibility that young men often feel, he may be strongly tempted to conclude that he can beat the odds. He might begin to think that if he and the girl are very careful, they might "get away with it," he may get to the point of giving in to peer pressure. When a young man's hormones are surging, it can be very tempting to see premarital sex as a "safe bet."

That's when the moral and spiritual realities that you have built into your son during The Talk will be invaluable. Because the whole purpose of The Talk is not to reinforce in your son the kind of thinking that says: What, exactly, are the risks? What can I possibly get away with? The Talk is about virtue, being a real man, a man who instead asks himself, What's the right thing to do? What would God have me do? What does godly obedience look like in this situation? What lines up with Scripture?

Birth Control and STDs

We already spent some time on STDs, but you can't discuss birth control responsibly without making some mention of disease as well. As is clear from the information above, birth control methods are awful at preventing STDs. Ironically, people who use birth control often feel their "protection," as flawed as it is, protects them against anything that could possibly go wrong, STDs included. While condoms are often touted as the "best" form of STD protection, they offer very little actual protection against some of the most prevalent and contagious STDs like HPV.

Help your son understand why a girl would choose to use a birth control method (such as the pill, the patch, or hormonal implants) that provides a degree of continual, day-in and day-out protection against pregnancy. Except for some rare medical conditions relating to female hormones, it is often because she wants to feel that it's "safe" to have sex any time she wishes,

146

with whomever she wishes. These young ladies have been sadly deceived into believing that they are now able to have "safe sex." Anyone who chooses to join those who are sexually active before marriage steps into the difficult world of STDs and teen pregnancy.

The bottom line is that birth control methods offer no true protection from STDs. Limiting yourself to oral sex is no prevention either, since STDs can be spread through oral sex as well. The only true protection from STDs is to live according to God's perfect plan for sexual activity—a man and a woman who have both rejected premarital sex get married, experience together all the beauties and joys of married, committed sex, and remain faithful for life. What a wonderful plan!

CHAPTER 11 QUESTIONS FOR DISCUSSING STDs AND BIRTH CONTROL

1. "Why do you think God made sex so appealing to men?"
2. "Do you know what a Sexually Transmitted Disease (STD) is?" "Can you name a few of them?"
3. "Do you know anyone who has an STD?" You probably do, you just don't know that they have the disease.
4. "What is "safe sex"?" "What makes sex "safe" versus "dangerous"?"
5. "Can you think of three good reasons not to have sex outside of God's plan for marriage?"
6. "Why do you suppose God instructs us not to have sex before we are married?"
7. "Who are you protecting by choosing not to have sex before marriage?" "How are you protecting them?"
8. Given how strong our natural desire to have sex is, can you see why it takes a true man not to give in to that temptation, choosing to follow God instead?
9. "Can you describe to me what abstinence is?" "What about the pill and how it works?"
10. "Which birth control methods are 100 percent effective?"

CHAPTER 12

Abuse and Abusers

Simply put, "abuse" happens when we fail to embrace biblical love. In fact, it's impossible to abuse someone and show biblical love at the same time.

I have heard 1 Corinthians 13:4–7 referred to as "the wedding verse" because it's present in so many wedding ceremonies—and rightfully so. In these verses God (who is love) provides us with his definition of love. In case you haven't been to a wedding in a while, here's a refresher:

> Love is patient, love is kind. It does not envy, it does not boast, it is not proud. It is not rude, it is not self-seeking, it is not easily angered, it keeps no record of wrongs. Love does not delight in evil but rejoices with the truth. It always protects, always trusts, always hopes, always perseveres. Love never fails.
> —1 Corinthians 13:4–8

Think about it. If everyone embraced these elements of love it would end abuse. I pray that more men would see these verses as their "life verses" that they recite daily rather than simply verses they hear when they happen to attend a wedding.

Abuse is a powerful example to show our sons that when we choose to turn from the clear, direct teaching of God's Word, bad things happen.

Abuse

We have already covered sexual perversions, but there are other types of perversion that you will need to discuss with your son. They are not necessarily sexual in nature, but they are perversions just the same. These perversions involve a range of behaviors and activities that come under the broad heading of abuse.

For some people, "abuse" sounds like it must involve drugs or alcohol. Others think first about physically abusive husbands or boyfriends. This chapter is about both categories, and more, because all forms of abuse have much in common.

Abuse, whatever form it takes, is simply a failure to embrace biblical love. It involves using something—such as a drug, your voice, or your strength—in ways not intended by God. Abuse is a failure of self-control, and often comes from feeling a loss of control. You can't handle or don't want to handle your emotions so you lash out, verbally or physically. You can't handle or don't want to handle a sense of pressure about what's wrong with your life, so you ingest too much of something in an effort to radically change the way you feel.

By definition, abuse is a perversion that causes harm to oneself or others. It is a pure negative. Your son needs to understand what abuse is, why it happens, and how he can discern it, avoid it, and prevent it. The Talk is your chance to tell him.

It Starts Early

No one grows up thinking he will become an abusive adult, or addicted to some substance. The path to abuse usually starts out

150

very simply, but then, one step at a time, you creep closer until one day you cross the line.

Displeasure becomes anger. Anger becomes yelling. Yelling becomes violence, and a wife has to call the police to intervene between her and the man she vowed to honor and obey. A bottle of beer becomes a shot of whiskey, then something else, and in what seems like no time at all an addiction has a young man contemplating suicide.

Obviously, not every difficult situation leads to a 911 call. Not everyone who drinks a beer will become an alcoholic, but this much is obvious: The sin patterns that lead a man to abuse are most often formed in his youth and young manhood. Add this, then, to your list of excellent reasons for being diligent in presenting The Talk to your son: It might just save his marriage, his career, or his life. Teach him to cultivate humility and the fruit of the Spirit (Galatians 5:22) now, and you greatly reduce the likelihood that abuse will ever control him.

In the following sections I outline some key facts on abuse that you will want to share with your son.

Abusive Behavior

Physical abuse involves any physical contact intended to cause injury, suffering, or harm. It's not always easy to identify, especially to a reluctant spouse who has become isolated. Even doctors and nurses are trained to identify signs of possible physical abuse. So it's important that your son understands where physical abuse begins.

Psychological abuse can take many forms, but for the sake of simplicity we will limit our discussion to probably its most common form, verbal abuse. This can be more difficult to identify than physical abuse. Verbal abuse can take the form of foul or offensive language—not hard to identify. In some cases, however, it may consist of repetitively degrading comments or even the "silent treatment" as a husband stubbornly refuses to say a single word to his wife.

You become verbally abusive, therefore, when your words (or silence) are meant to demean, punish, invoke anger, or humiliate. Like physical abuse, verbal abuse is often an attempt to force another person into submission.

Is all striking physical abuse? Is all forceful speech verbal abuse? No. It depends on your motivations. Spanking a young child can come from excellent motivations, with no desire to cause harm, and can produce an outcome that is good for all. When time is of the essence, forcefully raising your voice to get someone's attention quickly is not an effort to intimidate or harm, but to help. Many other examples could be given. The important point is your motivation: Are you doing this to help or to hurt; to build up, or tear down?

Substance Abuse

Paul exhorts the Ephesians to not be foolish but instead to understand what the Lord's will is. What does he say the Lord's will is? To not get drunk, but to instead be filled with the Spirit (Ephesians 5:17–18). He is telling us, your son included, not to participate in substance abuse of any kind but to trust him to give us freely everything we need.

Substance abuse is extremely common in our society and is based on nothing more than lies. "If you take this you will leave the emotional pain behind you." "If you snort that your sex life will improve." "If you don't participate you will be a loser, a chicken, an outcast," and the lies go on and on. The lie of substance abuse is that good things will happen when you stray from God. Without exception, pain and anguish will ultimately be the result.

Steroids are a great example. Scores of modern day "heroes" have made great strides in their sports and become rich and famous because of their steroid use. Olympic athletes, body builders, baseball players, football players, and the list goes on of those who are willing to cheat in order to be counted among the truly great athletes of our time.

152

"Everyone else is doing steroids," they reason. "It's my body so I can do what I want with it, anyway, I'm not hurting anybody." Then in humiliation those who are caught are deposed of their medals, their honors, and their highly esteemed place in both society and history.

Not everyone gets caught though, but their end is often times worse than those who do get busted. Many early steroid users found that their substance abuse had indeed affected others—like the wife who was crushed to find out that she will never experience the joy of giving birth because her rich and famous husband took steroids that made him sterile. Whether you are rich or poor, famous or not so famous, sooner or later the pain of abuse will deal a crushing blow.

Perhaps an example a little closer to home for your son is that of underage drinking. Underage and excessive drinking by young people is on the rise, and the use of illegal drugs is increasing, especially among young teens, but you can help. Teenagers whose parents talk to them regularly about the dangers of drugs are 42 percent less likely to use drugs than those whose parents don't.[4] The Talk is a great opportunity to have this conversation.

Appendix C has some basic facts about substance abuse to consider passing along to your son.

Abuse and the Virtuous Man

Everyone at some time is tempted to be physically or verbally abusive. When a man is abusive to his wife or girlfriend he has chosen to attack her, the weaker vessel, unmercifully, without regard for her well-being. He has become cowardly, proud, and selfish. He is anything but virtuous.

Many people can also be tempted to resort to substance abuse in an effort to feel better. The younger this begins, the more likely that addiction will set in, often permanently altering the course of one's life.

On the other hand, when a man chooses by God's grace to be self-controlled, he refuses to use tobacco, refrains from taking

153

drugs for non-medicinal purposes, does not abuse alcohol, does not use physical force in a relationship, and rejects the temptation to speak offensively, this is a man of godly virtue. He will be courageous enough to bear hardship without displays of anger and violence, and without escaping into substance abuse.

This is the man who will be counted among the noble and courageous. Remind your son of the man he can become, and make clear to him that avoiding the traps of physical, verbal, and substance abuse are key to his growing maturity. This should be the expectation you leave with your son. This and the good news that, no matter what sinful habits he may have already begun to develop, he can repent and see significant changes in his life with God's help.

CHAPTER 12 QUESTIONS FOR DISCUSSING ABUSE

1. "What are three types of abuse that a man must be careful not to get trapped by?"
2. "What is the most commonly used drug for teens?"
3. "Have you heard someone being verbally abusive?" "How did it make you feel?"
4. "How do the character traits of a true man (humility, courage, purity, faithfulness, selflessness, and self-control) help us avoid becoming ensnared by abusive behavior?"

CHAPTER 13

Work and Career

As I said earlier, The Talk is about more than one event; it's a series of conversations and a time of significant change in the father-son relationship. The Talk is also about more than the subjects of sex and self-control; it should cover at least two other vital areas: deciding what to do with your life, and choosing whom to marry. These will be our subjects for the next two chapters.

Nothing At All

It was a warm spring day. I woke up and got ready for work just like so many other days. I had breakfast with my wife and children, gave the usual hugs and kisses before leaving for work, and out the door I went. When I got to work, I set about accomplishing all the tasks that were before me. I had a business to transition to another organization, figures to verify, papers and thoughts to pull together, and I needed to get everything in order for an important meeting the following morning.

I had a publication to review and give my approval of before sending it off to print. I had a number of calls to make concerning the renovation of our courtyard which was to begin in just a few days. I had just enough time before two very important meetings to stop at the cafeteria and pick up a little something to eat . . . of course I got it "to go."

It was there that I met Miss B. That's what she called herself, because that is what her mother called her—B. Miss B was a slightly stooped, small black lady with gray hair. A large handbag constantly slipped off the shoulder of her rose-colored rain coat that she wore on this sunny spring day.

She was looking for her physician's office and had inadvertently entered the wrong building. I told Miss B that I would walk her to the building she was looking for, as it was on my way. Miss B struck up a conversation as she shuffled slowly down the long corridor. People walking at a normal pace seemed to run past us as I tried to adjust to her speed. I was frustrated that I had to go so slow. As you recall, I had a lot to accomplish in one eight-hour day.

Miss B told me that she was from North Carolina and that she had worked in the shipyards for years. She told me that she was eighty-six years old and that God had blessed her. She gave me some advice, "Do good to others and God will bless you," she said matter-of-factly. Miss B told me that she married a man from Windsor, Virginia. She told me about the time that her Momma gave her "what for" when she had her hair cut without permission. She blessed her mother. I learned that she had volunteered at a local church, for years untold, until she just couldn't do it anymore.

Miss B had outlived her brothers and sisters and now the old home where she was born had been left to her. I could see in her eyes that she was only half pleased with the inheritance. I think she knew that the home wasn't "the home" without the others and it was, therefore, a hollow thing to her now.

Miss B only schooled until the ninth grade, but she was smart and she knew it. I knew it too. We walked to her building and

156

she stopped to tell me a little more about herself. She looked me in my white face and said, "Black or white it's all the same to God you know."

She asked me what I did and I told her. I'm sure she didn't understand what I said. "Do your work well," she advised me, "and you'll be respected by everyone." She understood more than I gave her credit for.

I spent all of ten minutes with Miss B. I said goodbye and we wished each other a good day. She went to her appointment and I went back to my business. As I opened the door to my office, I realized that for the last ten minutes I had accomplished nothing at all.

I paused. After I thought for a moment, I realized that those last ten minutes would be the most important ten minutes of my day.

Some fine advice from a stranger and here's some for you. A discussion on work may seem, well, less important than the other topics covered in The Talk. Don't be fooled, sometimes the most benefit is received from the most unexpected of places. There's a reason that God included work as part of the creation mandate—because it plays an important role in our ability to glorify God and enjoy him forever. Your son's work ethic will affect every part of his life. As you will see, it's not so much what he chooses to do, as much as it is how he chooses to do it. You're helping him work on his heart and he needs to get it straight from the start. This is your opportunity to help guide him along his way.

Gifts and Interests

Even if your son is young, your first time having The Talk with him will be a great opportunity to begin a discussion about making a living. Start by talking about the things he likes to do.

God gives each of us gifts, talents, and strengths, and these are nearly always reflected in the things we enjoy. Activities that bring us satisfaction are often signposts directing us toward a certain kind of work. The path to a man's eventual career may be long and winding, including the occasional false turn and dead end. Upon finally arriving at a satisfying career, he will usually recognize how childhood passions for a certain activity or subject have led him to where he is. It's usually better to recognize those passions earlier in life rather than later.

We live in a day when it is far easier than in the past for a man to work in an area of particular strength and enjoyment. Nearly vanished are the days when career options were driven almost entirely by where you lived or who your parents were. In decades past, for example, men became farmers because their family owned a farm, or spent their whole lives on an assembly line because that was the biggest industry in town. Surely in many cases these men were not in vocations that played to their strengths. The economic and social structures simply chose a vocation for them. This has been true for most of the men who have ever lived, but not anymore. It's likely that your son will have an opportunity relatively rare in human history—to choose a career that emphasizes his particular talents and gifts.

Start this part of The Talk by probing around, asking about your son's areas of interest until you find something that he thinks he might like to do vocationally. Does he like computer games? Sports? Crime novels? Drawing? No matter what he comes up with, as long as it is legal, moral, and ethical, don't discourage it. The important thing about this discussion is to get your son thinking about the future and to tie the idea of personal passions to the idea of vocation.

Suppose your son enjoys playing computer games. Does he think he might want to design such games for a living? Draw him out about it. Be encouraging and help him start thinking in new ways. "I think you could be a really good game designer. What is it about gaming that you like so much? What types of games would be your favorite to write? Did you know that designing games is very similar to writing novels? You need a plot, some twists, things that are difficult to figure out, and all the while you need to keep the user entertained. If you were going to be the greatest game designer who ever lived, how would you need to prepare?"

Not all young men, whatever their age during The Talk, will be able to speak with any clarity or conviction about what they want to do when they grow up, or how to get there. That's not a problem. There is time for all these things to be clarified. The important thing is to get your son thinking about the idea of a life direction and the development of excellence. In having a conversation like this with your son, you will be:

- encouraging him about his passions
- learning more about what he enjoys
- hearing his early thoughts, if any, about a possible vocation
- giving him new tools for thinking about his own future
- helping him see that the options may be greater than he had imagined
- planting seeds for the pursuit of God-glorifying excellence

Work as a Joy

There is a place in every man's life, or perhaps a number of places, where gifts and calling and enjoyment can come together to produce excellence. Martin Luther King, Jr. made an inspiring point about the value of being excellent in your work and the holiness of having a sense of calling. "If a man is called to be a street sweeper, he should sweep streets even as Michelangelo painted, or Beethoven played music, or Shakespeare wrote poetry. He should sweep streets so well that all the hosts of heaven and earth will pause to say, here lived a great street sweeper who did his job well."

Whatever your son does, he should decide to become the best that he can possibly be at it. Remind him it was God who gave him his abilities and desires in the first place. Tell him he will be spending the majority of his life working, and that merely having a large income is rarely enough to sustain a man happily if he doesn't enjoy his work. In fact, a man's work should be so important to him that he will push himself to be the best at it every day of his life.

If you can set your son on a path to discerning a vocation he will love, you will have done him a great service. Ultimately he will make his own decisions, but to get him thinking squarely about what is important will put him miles ahead of other young men.

Competition Starts Now

Contrary to what may be taught in public school systems, competition is alive and well in the world of work and business. Whatever a man's field, advancement and success are directly tied to his ability to rise above those around him by taking initiative and performing his work with excellence.

Going back to the idea of being a video game designer, if that is what your son wants he must consider what he must do to become better at it than the other sons and daughters who also want to be game designers. What does he need to learn and do to sell his idea over the ideas of others? Does he love the idea of game design enough to work long and hard to become the best at it?

Whether a street sweeper or a CEO, you cannot be the best at what you do without studying how others perform that kind of work, and then determining to do it better. That's competition. In every area of his life—whether vocation, marriage, or sport—your son should purpose to rise to the top of his abilities.

Riches and Virtue

Recent research on millionaires who have maintained healthy marriages and well-rounded lives reveals some interesting patterns. What makes the wealthiest of the wealthy different? What gives them the ability to create wealth more effectively than others? What allows them to succeed in multiple areas of their lives where others often struggle or fail? Here are some factors not on the list: superior education, growing up in a wealthy family, inheriting wealth, or winning the lottery.

Far more significant to becoming successful in the broadest sense are these key factors: honesty in all your dealings, being

160

able to take risks and overcome obstacles, keeping your family a top priority in your thinking and planning, and a desire and willingness to work harder than others. In other words, honesty, courage, faithfulness, integrity, selflessness, and diligence. Here is how to view these character traits in terms of excellence and competition:

Honesty

Having a proven track record of being forthright with others, and therefore trusted to deal fairly in all matters.

Courage

Being willing to step into a position of uncertainty and risk based on analysis and a reasonable belief that success may be attainable. This is often a matter of not waiting for a clear path, but making one. Courage becomes especially important when the situation has a moral context and there is a particular risk associated with doing the right thing.

Selflessness

Vocational aims must not compromise a man's love for and service to his family. He should do his work for his family, rather than sacrifice his family for his work.

Diligence

Working hard and being genuinely devoted to one's work means that a man needs to enjoy what he does for a living, so that enjoyment can fuel his diligence.

These aren't an exact match to the biblical virtues we studied in chapter 4 (humility, courage, faithfulness, selflessness, and self-control), but they are certainly in the same ball park and made of the same godly stuff. The fact is, the more virtuous your son is, the more likely he is to create and retain wealth while keeping the rest of his life in balance.

The Thing about Education

With all that said, how is your son to think about his education if he wants to be the best he can possibly be? Does all this mean he needs to strive for an Ivy-League or some other expensive and intensive college experience? How should a formal education be viewed with respect to vocation, money, and your son's future? What if your son isn't the valedictorian type? What if he is basically a "C" student? Is he destined to work on road crews all his life? In other words, does more education always translate to more overall life success?

Personally, as someone with a graduate degree, I believe that the notion of higher education being a ticket to true success is highly overrated. Certainly it equips and trains many people in ways they could not otherwise be, but this is hardly a guarantee of any particular outcome. Many college graduates work in fields completely unrelated to their majors. And for those who do actually put their degree to use, many top-of-the-class college grads work their entire careers for college dropouts—people who have learned how to leverage their personal strengths and the efforts of others to propel themselves to wealth and success. In fact, a reliance on grades and standardized tests can lull valedictorian types into a false vision of certain prosperity.

Education is important, but it must be put in perspective. It is not a one-size-fits-all solution. It is a tool—one among many—that can help a virtuous young man reach his goals and succeed in his life. Note the emphasis here on an individual's goals and an individual's life. In many cases, of course, men work within organizations that to a large degree set goals for them. Help your son to think these things through. There is nothing wrong with working in an honorable job for an organization, large or small, that does honorable work. However, given the changes in technology, society, and the economy in recent years, the long-term security of these positions has substantially decreased, and the opportunity to work outside these positions has substantially increased.

If you are considering college for your son, encourage him during his sophomore year in high school to try to formulate and write down his goals for his college education and vocation. He may not have a very clear picture of his future, but at least he will be thinking about it and focusing on it, which will be far more than most of his peers are doing. Your encouragement will help him root his planning and thinking in what is important to him, so that what he learns and how he grows in college will be of real value to him. Help him to recognize that God has placed a rich potential for excellence within him, but that he will not attain it unless he sets a high standard for himself.

Above all, communicate to your son that reaching his goals and becoming a true success begins and ends with his ability to be humble, courageous, pure, faithful, selfless, and self-controlled. If he is going to succeed in ways that please God and truly matter, he must first choose to be virtuous.

Becoming a Confidant

After this portion of The Talk, your son should be excited about the prospects before him. He should realize now that, with a little bit of foresight and a whole lot of hard work, true excellence and great accomplishments—everything God is calling him to in this life—are within his grasp.

Now you have affirmed that your son has gifts and abilities. You have also demonstrated your understanding of how different factors combine to influence the course of a man's life. As a result, your son will be much more likely to confide in you when considering important educational and career decisions. You are becoming the trusted confidant you set out to become at the start.

CHAPTER 13 QUESTIONS FOR DISCUSSING WORK

1. Name three ways that God has gifted you?
2. "What careers would you say those gifts might be effectively used in?"

3. "If you could pick any career you wanted today, what would you choose?"

4. "Is the concept of working more of a joy or a dread to you?" "Do you think God created us for joy or dread?" "How then should we view our work?"

5. "How can your gifts be aligned with what brings you joy, to create a career path that will allow you to delight in your work?"

CHAPTER 14

Considering a Wife

A Little Help from Our Friends

I was twenty-eight when I met my wife, and she was twenty-seven. It was the first time I ever considered getting married, but I really felt that it was my time. My wife was beautiful, fun, smart, and so easy to talk to. Not only that, but she wanted children just like I did. To me it seemed like a perfect match—if she would have me.

Thankfully, we were part of a strong local church that helped us wade through the decision-making process. We never attended "marriage classes," but we both desired to have a few individuals from the church weigh in on our relationship. In our case these were lay leaders who were well established in the church and with whom we already had a strong relationship. We gave them the freedom to speak into our lives so that we would be able to make a wise decision concerning our relationship. Take note that my wife and I always retained the responsibility of making our own decision. We took some advice and put other advice aside as we saw fit, but giving those Christian men and women the freedom to speak into our lives was the wisest thing we ever did as two single adults.

We dated initially by seeing each other in group settings. We continued seeking counsel and saw each other in group settings, but now and again on our own we would go to dinner or a movie, or to the park and our relationship continued to blossom.

Thankfully, she accepted my proposal and in a little over a year we were married. Of course I had both churched and un-churched friends and the response from the two groups when they heard I was engaged was very telling.

From the church I received strong encouragement. I heard statements like, "Marriage is hard work, but it's the best decision you'll ever make," and "I'm so happy for you; your life is about to change for the better; marriage is great."

From my un-churched friends I heard statements like, "Man, you just ruined your life," and "You had it made, you could see as many girls as you wanted and now you're getting married?"

I thank God for my church family as well as the support from my immediate family. How grateful I am even these twenty-three years later that I had a strong Christian fellowship to help me keep my relationship pure and that I received the good counsel and encouragement that confirmed God's call to my wife and me.

Immediately after our honeymoon we entered into our next life adventure as a team—we moved from Ohio to Virginia to be part of a church planting team. God has been so gracious to us both.

A Course-Setting Decision

Two decisions in a man's life set his course more permanently and more profoundly than any others he will ever make: Will I follow Christ? and Whom shall I marry?

We have already discussed the gospel in some detail, so in this chapter we will consider the second. After you have covered the other subjects in The Talk, you need to turn your son's attention to the day when he starts to think about getting married.

This is not a matter of telling your son how to choose a wife. In keeping with the spirit of The Talk, it's about offering him information and ways of thinking that will serve him as he matures, and will promote a deeper and richer father-son relationship.

Reality Check

Your son must understand that for every moral threat you have warned him about, young women face a similar threat. Abuse and abusers, sexual sin and its ramifications, pressure from the world to conform to sinful habits—all these threats are equally real for young ladies, just in somewhat different ways.

One day your son will consider a particular young woman as a marriage partner. You will do him a great service if you prepare him now for a reality check: However beautiful, innocent, and spiritually deep this young lady may appear, she too has spent her entire life as a sinner in a fallen world, subject to continual temptations and moral dangers. Where might she have stumbled? What particular weaknesses and temptations does she carry in her heart?

The idea is not to suggest to your son that he should keep searching until he finds a perfect woman. For one thing, there aren't any. Besides, your son is not a perfect man. Rather, your son will one day need to find the woman who is right for him, just as he is right for her, with neither of them being perfect people.

Because all of us are fallen, a vitally important part of marriage is exercising grace, humility, and faith toward your spouse in the face of temptations, weaknesses, and sin. How can your son know if a particular young lady might bring habits, sins, or experiences into a marriage that could greatly complicate their life together? He has to be willing to ask.

It is beyond the scope of this book to discuss the process of premarital counseling, but let me be clear, it may not be best for your son and an attractive young woman to go off by themselves and discuss the most intimate details of their lives. There may well need to be older adults involved, perhaps at times even serving as intermediaries between your son and his potential spouse. However the process works, the topics appearing below need to be addressed—and handled with humility, grace, wisdom, and careful timing.

Of course, throughout this process your son will need to be open, as well. The goal is complete transparency by both young people. If either cannot be completely forthcoming and honest, they are probably not ready for marriage.

Here are some areas that will be important to address.

Salvation

If your son is a Christian, then the Word of God and the collective wisdom of generations of Christians before him suggest one thing clearly. The woman he chooses to be his wife should be a Christian as well (see 2 Corinthians 6:14–17). Indeed, she should have a personal and growing relationship with the Savior, Jesus.

A difference in faith may appear a small thing at first, but it will certainly become increasingly difficult to reconcile over time. It cannot help but to become a bone of contention in a marriage relationship, especially when children come into the picture. Mark Dever makes a strong case for following this biblical command:

> If you are engaged to a non-Christian, break off the engagement. . . . Better to lose your deposits on receptions and invitations than your soul. "Are you saying that I can lose my salvation by marrying a non-Christian?" No, I am saying that your actions reveal what you really love. . . . God has a wonderful plan for us in marriage, and part of it includes finding someone with whom we can establish a peaceful unity, where we reinforce one another, not where we disagree and chafe over the matters that we claim are closest to our hearts.

Suppose your son comes home from his first year away at college and announces that he has met the woman of his dreams and he hopes to propose to her before the end of the summer—and she's not a Christian. What would you do? What should you do?

Your son is nineteen years old and you have met his girlfriend. She is attractive, well-mannered, soft-spoken and a lot of fun to be around. She is also an atheist. Here are your options:

1. Forbid him to see her again because she's not a Christian.
2. Tell his girlfriend in confidence that he can only marry a Christian.
3. Close your mouth and hope for the best.
4. Tell them both about God's rule that Christians can only marry another Christian.
5. Take time to discuss the implications of marrying an unbeliever with your son, together seeking to hear the Lord's call on his life and encourage him to seek counsel from other trusted leaders in the church.

You would be surprised how many fathers without thinking choose numbers 1–4 and create years of strife in their homes. In our zeal for wanting what's best for our sons we sometimes forget that the decision is his to make and that we are only counselors. If we have built a strong relationship with our son over time, and if we are part of a strong local church, then our counsel will hold more weight.

Regardless of whether your son believes the woman he would like to pursue is a Christian or not, he should seek counsel from others before making any kind of a commitment. First, if your relationship is strong, he should approach you. Then he should consult leaders in his church who he knows and whose opinions he values and trusts to help him in his discernment.

There is wisdom in a multitude of counselors and who your son marries will be one of the biggest decisions of his life.

Sexual Activity

As discussed earlier, any history of sexual contact prior to marriage carries the risk of bringing disease into a marriage. Choosing whether or not to marry a woman with an STD is your son's choice, but you can help him make sure he doesn't find out too late. If your son or his girlfriend has been sexually active, it would be worth getting medically tested for STDs before setting a wedding date.

If sexual perversion has been a factor, it can be a difficult bondage to break free from. The effects on a man or woman can last a lifetime. If your son's potential spouse has experimented with homosexuality or any other sexual perversion, this should be made clear and the implications considered carefully prior to making a lifelong commitment.

Abusive Past

As we have seen, abuse can take many forms: physical, verbal, or psychological, and one I have not yet specifically mentioned, sexual abuse. Abuse in any form can have deep and lasting effects. Some people, despite being out from under the influence of an abusive situation, may still carry emotional or physical scars for the rest of their lives. In most situations love will overcome these obstacles, and even help to heal them, but to be surprised by such news after a year of marriage can be devastating.

Drugs and Alcohol

Experience with drugs and/or alcohol is increasingly common among young people. Even being in a "good family" or a "good church" is no sure safeguard against such activities. No matter how temporary or fleeting such experiences may have been, they need to be disclosed.

Mental Illness

Many mental illnesses are fully controllable with proper medication. Some, however, bring a volatility or unpredictability that can destroy a marriage. A strong spouse may be able to extend grace where the effectiveness of medication falls somewhat short, but even that is likely to become extremely difficult year after year. Certainly this is an area that should be disclosed. If there is such a history, in addition to speaking with his father, it would also be wise to speak with a pastor, and perhaps with someone who has been married to a person with a similar mental illness. A realistic picture of what this is like will be invaluable to making an informed decision.

Medications

There are many reasons someone might be taking medications: Allergies, chronic illness, depression, pain, and on and on. When your son knows his potential spouse's medications, he will be better able to discern what she is dealing with, and how he may be called upon to serve her in the future.

Full Disclosure

I am not suggesting an interrogation proceeding or a clinical checklist approach. I am, however, strongly encouraging wisdom and extreme caution when any of these things are brought into a relationship. Teens simply don't have the foresight or experience to comprehend the implications of disease and past experiences on a relationship. They can barely understand what it means to make a lifelong commitment and live it out—but you understand.

Don't assume. Tell your son directly that while the decisions a man makes are his own, that you would certainly help him walk through significant decisions like marriage. Further encourage him to build strong relationships within your local church so that he will have other trusted people to turn to for wise counsel whenever he needs it. Teach him that there is indeed wisdom in a multitude of counselors, and that he needs to prepare now by building those relationships with strong Christian men who will be able to give him sound advice when the time comes.

In the end, your son will make his own decision and you will love and support him, his spouse, and your grandchildren 100 percent. For now, it is your responsibility to be clear about these matters with your son, even if he is the one with the disease or the questionable background. You promised him at the outset full disclosure and no excuses. Now is the time to live up to your word.

CHAPTER 14 QUESTIONS FOR CONSIDERING A WIFE

1. "Do you think you will ever get married?"
2. "Why do you think God is so adamant about marrying another Christian?"
3. "What do you think is the best way to find out about your prospective wife's past?"
4. "Why would you want to find out all this personal information before getting married?" "Is it really that important?"

PART 4

Conclusion

CHAPTER 15

Three Final Truths

We have finished our discussion about how to present The Talk. In this closing chapter I want to leave you with some perspective on what to do, and what to expect after having presented The Talk for the first time. I will try to underscore and draw some implications from three overarching truths.

1. The Talk is not magic; no matter how effective your talk is, your son will still sin.
2. The Talk will usually change the father-son relationship forever. So live like things are different—because they probably are.
3. Through it all, trust in, rely on, and most of all, pray unceasingly; The Talk is only effective to the extent that your heart and your communication are in line with God's Word and his ways.

The Wisdom of Age

When I was a young man I spent a year in Greece, on the Island of Crete, helping my Great-Uncle Andreas who was eighty-seven years old at the time. Great-Uncle Andreas lived in a small mountain village in a home that his father had built over one hundred years before. To say that it was a rustic mountain home is an understatement. There was neither electricity nor running water when I lived there, and the floor of the home was the top of the mountain—rocks, craters and all.

I often walked with my great-uncle to the village center where people would sometimes congregate, play backgammon or cards and generally socialize. One day, while walking to the center, Andreas looked me square in the face and asked, "When you go to the village, do you speak with the girls?" This was kind of surprising since there were only two girls of my age in this small village of seventy or so people.

"Yes, sometimes," I replied.

"Don't talk to the girls in the village," Andreas commanded curtly. "These people can be a little crazy here."

My thought was that my uncle was surely thinking as if we were still in the late 1800s when it was not proper in Greece for men to speak socially with a young lady. I was soon to find out that I was wrong, and the discounting of my great-uncle's wisdom could cost me dearly.

One evening in late summer a political rally was held in our village. Over one hundred people flocked into Malaxa from adjoining villages to hear the candidate speak. After the rally, the people mulled about having sometimes heated conversations concerning their political views. Amidst one argument, a man turned to me, pulled a handgun out of his coat and jokingly said, "This is for her, since she is for the other party." He thought it funny, but I thought it time to leave, and I did so promptly. It was well after dark and on my way back to my great-uncle's home I met up with one of the girls from the village who was standing at the fork in the road.

"Meet me at the ruins," she said, "and we will have some time to talk." Under normal circumstances I would have agreed in a heartbeat. I was twenty-five years old after all, and she was very attractive at twenty-one. However, having just come from the gun-toting, politically charged rally, I graciously refused, saying something to the effect that I was not able to speak with her in the daytime, much less at night, and begged her pardon as I continued to my room to enjoy a good night's sleep.

In the morning I woke up and walked to the other side of the village to my Great-Aunt Crystalo's home for breakfast. To my surprise she echoed the same question that Andreas had asked weeks before: "Are you speaking with the girls in the village?"

"Well, yes," I replied, "but not when I'm with Uncle Andreas." The explanation that followed reoriented me to the understanding of age and wisdom, and completely changed my perception of my elders.

"Don't talk to the girls in this village," she began. "My friend was just here and told me that there is a plan to catch you alone with one of the girls and to force you to marry her."

"Whoa," I thought, "this information is just a bit late, as the snare had been set at the fork in the road, after the political rally just the night before." Despite my disobedience to my great-uncle's good counsel, by grace I was spared from a serious predicament—being the main attraction at an old-fashioned shotgun wedding in Malaxa on the Island of Crete. Needless to say, from that point, on I listened much more intently to the instructions of my great-uncle, recognizing and heeding his good counsel.

While it is true that I learned a good lesson, I hope that you will be able to gain from this experience as well. At the time, I did not accept the good counsel from my great-uncle, I was simply too wise in my own eyes. Despite my disobedience, Andreas did not give up on me. He did not get angry and stop giving his advice. He never expected me to take his advice or thought bad of me for ignoring it. He never harped and rarely repeated counsel once given.

Over time, wisdom will always be proved right. My Great-Uncle Andreas was both patient and unassuming. He seemed to understand that it was not his responsibility to make me understand, but only to share his advice with me. Young people will make their mistakes, but with the help of a faithful father your son may be able to avoid some of the mistakes that would otherwise cost him greatly.

The bottom line is that your son needs your wisdom, although he may not yet recognize it as such. Don't get frustrated if your advice is not taken. Remember: in time, wisdom will always be proved right.

I thank God for my Great-Uncle Andreas. Although I didn't meet him until he was over eighty years old, he greatly impacted my life. I will be forever grateful for the patience he had with me, and the wisdom he shared when I was still way too wise in my own eyes to receive it.

No Miracles, No Magic

As much as we might wish otherwise, The Talk cannot inoculate our sons against foolishness and sin. It is not a magic wand that, if we wave it just the right way, will secure the future.

Fathers are responsible before God for training and guiding their sons, and The Talk is an absolutely critical component of that process. While this is true, the reality is that your son is going to make his own decisions and will one day answer to God as an individual. It's his life, and he will travel his own path and make his own mistakes. Just like you have.

I have seen parents, bound up in pride and legalism, who actually disowned their children when they made bad, sinful decisions. How could this come as such a surprise to a father? Is his own childhood forgotten so quickly? Does he really imagine that somehow his son is not subject to the temptations that are common to man (see 1 Corinthians 10:13)?

Weathering the Perfect Storm

This takes us back to a point made much earlier. Why is it so important to begin The Talk when your son is at a fairly young age? Because soon after that several things will come together in his life.

- He will grow physically and mentally stronger.
- He will become increasingly tempted by the ways of the world.

- He will gradually gain independence, and will be tempted to desire more than what is best for him to have.
- He will want to scale new peaks of personal accomplishment, to master new challenges, to put fresh notches in his belt.
- He will become more concerned with his reputation among his peers.

This is the perfect storm of circumstances that sends the lives of so many young men careening off a godly course, often for years, sometimes forever. As your son becomes a young man you will not be able to stop him from taking his own way, but when, through The Talk, you prepare him for what is surely coming, then the two of you, together, will be far better equipped to help him weather the storm and stay on course, more or less (again, do not expect perfection!).

Will you be there to help your son get back on course when he realizes his mistakes? You can be. The Talk may not be a magic wand, but if you commit to doing it right, it is a nearly certain guarantee of creating a much stronger, deeper father-son relationship.

Live Like Things Are Different

Once you have completed the first session of The Talk, what's next? Schedule the second session. If your son was really ready for the first, it will probably be best to schedule a follow-up for six or eight months down the road. If a third session turns out to be necessary, the same six-to-eight-month interim is probably about right; once your son becomes tuned in to this subject matter you may be surprised at how quickly he matures.

Also be alert for those daily conversations that can pop up at unexpected times. Once you have opened the door to discussing somewhat intimate matters with your son, don't pretend nothing has changed. On any given day, you may find yourself in conversations about manhood that could never have happened prior to The Talk.

Remember, change takes time. You have just planted the seed so you may not see it sprouting just yet. Let me encourage you to live like things are different, because they probably are. Look for practical ways to treat your son more like a man. Encourage him in his decision-making and continue to discern when to be a friend and counselor instead of the "boss." Some of these things will be brief and simple, while others may get fairly long and complex. Of course, that's what it's all about—establishing an open channel of communication between father and son. With that in place, your son never needs to be in the dark. Whether you are a phone call away or right there in the house with him, he will always have access to a listening ear and a wealth of good counsel.

When those spontaneous moments arise, stop whatever else you are doing and give your full attention to your son. If he wants to talk on a weeknight, forty-five minutes after you had hoped to get to bed, sit down and talk. If he calls you at work, set aside your other priorities and focus on him.

At these moments, like no others, he is receptive to your input. Let him lead the conversation and give him your counsel, not your orders. Be an encouragement to him. If you shut him down, talk down to him, or talk at him, he may be less likely to continue confiding in you. Don't be caught off guard if his questions and concerns seem to come from deep left field. Your relationship needs to be a safe place for him to discuss all kinds of thoughts and topics, no matter how odd they may seem to you.

I assure you that some of your words to your son will be discarded. This is to be expected. So remember that this is about counsel, not command. Not only are you not God, you are not called to enforce God's requirements—he alone is Judge. Your son is becoming his own man. Let him do that. Your goal is not for your son to live your life, but his. Yet how much more stable, how much richer and more rewarding that life can be, now that you are building a loving, open, and honest relationship with him.

Pray Unceasingly

Raising boys is no simple task. There are no shortcuts, no easy paths, and no guarantees. In the process of raising my four boys

I've made lots of mistakes. At times I've been too demanding, at other times too lenient. I've made difficult decisions based on what I thought would be best, only to look back and wonder if I was right. Launching my sons to independence is one of the most difficult challenges I have ever faced.

How grateful we fathers should be that we can lean on the Lord, casting our fears, concerns, and anxieties upon him! Let us remember that our sons are his before they are ours. In the end it is the Lord who fights our battles and our sons' battles, for all this is about him, from beginning to end.

Therefore, I'm convinced that the best thing a father can do for his son is to pray for him. Pray unceasingly. Pray for his wife-to-be, for his children-to-be, for his integrity, for his purity, and especially for the Lord to draw your son to himself.

Despite our shortcomings as fathers, or the sins that our sons might willingly walk into along the way, we can pray for our sons even as the apostle Paul prayed for his children in Christ, the Philippians.

I thank my God every time I remember you. In all my prayers for all of you, I always pray with joy because of your partnership in the gospel from the first day until now, being confident of this, that he who began a good work in you will carry it on to completion until the day of Christ Jesus.

It is right for me to feel this way about all of you, since I have you in my heart; for whether I am in chains or defending and confirming the gospel, all of you share in God's grace with me. God can testify how I long for all of you with the affection of Christ Jesus.

And this is my prayer: that your love may abound more and more in knowledge and depth of insight, so that you may be able to discern what is best and may be pure and blameless until the day of Christ, filled with the fruit of righteousness that comes through Jesus Christ—to the glory and praise of God.

—Philippians 1:3–11

No Better Investment

When you consider the effort that goes into preparing and giving The Talk to your son, and then weigh the lifelong results, it's about the lowest-cost, highest-return investment one can possibly imagine. It's been quite a few years since I had my first talk with my oldest son, now twenty-one, but the dividends just keep paying out. Not long ago, I was able sit down and talk with him and his girlfriend about purity and their relationship. How many dads can venture into those waters expecting to make a catch? Will he be honest and forthright? Will he fall into sin and temptation? Those are decisions your son will have to make, but at least as a father you have given your son every opportunity to live a holy and righteous life that is blessed by God.

For all practical purposes, my oldest son is an adult who makes his own decisions. I have watched him make both good and bad ones, but we both know that the door we stepped through together those many years ago is still wide open. We know our relationship will remain strong through the years because of the foundation we set when he was still a young man.

Apart from God and my wife, the relationships I have built and am building with my children are the most precious, enduring, and rewarding in my life. I truly believe that any Christian father who implements The Talk with faith, prayer, and careful preparation can have a similar experience. Not because I said so—but because it's a clear, simple, effective way for a father to honor God and take Scripture seriously.

―――

My son, do not forget my teaching, but keep my commands in your heart, for they will prolong your life many years and bring you prosperity. Let love and faithfulness never leave you; bind them around your neck, write them on the tablet of your heart. Then you will win favor and a good name in the sight of God and man.
—Proverbs 3:1–4

Outline of The Talk

There is no typical pattern for giving The Talk. In fact, while I encourage you to come fully prepared with an outline like this one, first and foremost you must trust the Lord to lead you through this discussion. Sway from the outline as the Holy Spirit leads you to, after all, Jesus himself said that he was sending the Holy Spirit to lead us in the way of all truth.

This outline is provided only as a quick and easy reminder of topics. Use the check boxes to note which topics have been covered.

This list is by no means comprehensive. The Talk you give to your son is your own, so it is up to you to explain each topic in the detail you deem necessary and in your own words.

Starting Out

Let your son know how important he is to you.

Pray for him, for your time together, for the ministering of the Holy Spirit.

☐ 1. Much More Than a Talk

Every boy walks through this process.

You are becoming a young man now.

Outward (physical) changes are signs of a boy starting to mature.

I have brought you here to discuss things that are reserved for men to discuss.

You can ask any question.

I will be completely honest.

I will not hide anything from you that is appropriate for a man of your years.

I will answer all of your questions as best I can.

This discussion is meant for men of honor and is to be kept between men of honor.

Many of the things you have seen and heard about girls and men are not true.

☐ 2. The Culture Clash

Review the wheat and the tares.

Teach from the wheat.

God is central to the maturing process.

Virtuous men are rare today, but you can be one.

Despite what today's culture might tell you it is never healthy for boys to experiment with sexual indulgence and perversions.

☐ 3. Manhood As Designed By God

Created for work "God took the man and put him in the Garden of Eden to work it and take care of it" (Genesis 2:15).

Created for sexual pleasure according to God's plan (Be fruitful and multiply).

Created for family (a suitable helper).

Created to be obedient to God (You must not eat of the tree of the knowledge of good and evil).

Ultimately created for the Glory of God.

☐ 4. The Virtues of Manhood

☐ *Humility*

Pursuing humility means accepting the fact that your knowledge and abilities are limited, so in light of that, be wise and regularly seek help and graciously accept advice and even correction.

- This is the one I esteem: he who is humble and contrite in spirit, and trembles at my word (Isaiah 66:2).
- All of you, clothe yourselves with humility toward one another, because, "God opposes the proud but gives grace to the humble" (1 Peter 5:5).
- Humility and the fear of the LORD bring wealth and honor and life (Proverbs 22:4).

☐ *Courage*

To pursue courage means choosing to do what is right despite opposition from others or even opposition from your own desires (often the most difficult enemy to fight).

- Be on your guard; stand firm in the faith; be men of courage; be strong (1 Corinthians 16:13).
- So keep up your courage, men, for I have faith in God that it will happen just as he told me (Acts 27:25).
- Act with courage, and may the LORD be with those who do well (2 Chronicles 19:11).

185

☐ *Purity*

To pursue moral purity means choosing to live by the highest moral principles in your speech, actions, and physical relations, despite your own desires to do otherwise, and despite any kind of external pressure to compromise.

- How can a young man keep his way pure? By living according to your word (Psalm 119:9).
- Treat younger men as brothers, older women as mothers, and younger women as sisters, with absolute purity (1 Timothy 5:1–2).
- Set an example for the believers in speech, in life, in love, in faith and in purity (1 Timothy 4:12).
- Do not be hasty in the laying on of hands, and do not share in the sins of others. Keep yourself pure (1 Timothy 5:22).

☐ *Faithfulness*

To pursue faithfulness means acting in integrity, keeping your word, and doing what is right according to God's word, with fortitude and without complaining, because you are trusting God to give you the ability to complete all that he has given you to do.

- So then, men ought to regard us as servants of Christ and as those entrusted with the secret things of God. Now it is required that those who have been given a trust must prove faithful (1 Corinthians 4:1–2).
- Love the LORD, all his saints! The LORD preserves the faithful, but the proud he pays back in full. Be strong and take heart, all you who hope in the LORD (Psalm 31:23–24).
- A faithful man will be richly blessed (Proverbs 28:20).

☐ *Selflessness*

To pursue selflessness means placing the well-being of others before your own needs and desires.

- An unfriendly man pursues selfish ends; he defies all sound judgment (Proverbs 18:1).
- Do nothing out of selfish ambition or vain conceit, but in humility consider others better than yourselves. Each of you should look not only to your own interests, but also to the interests of others (Philippians 2:2–4).
- For where you have envy and selfish ambition, there you find disorder and every evil practice (James 3:16).

☐ *Self-control*

To pursue self-control means maintaining full presence of mind in all situations and circumstances, and choosing to exercise restraint despite your desire or tendency to do otherwise.

- Be self-controlled and alert. Your enemy the devil prowls around like a roaring lion looking for someone to devour (1 Peter 5:8).
- Like a city whose walls are broken down is a man who lacks self-control (Proverbs 25:28).
- But the fruit of the Spirit is love, joy, peace, patience, kindness, goodness, faithfulness, gentleness and self-control. Against such things there is no law (Galatians 5:22–23).

☐ 5. Beginning the Talk

- Check your attitude and expectations.
- You are coming into a new time in your life. You are beginning the journey from being a boy to becoming a man.
- Every boy walks through this process. Millions of guys have already done this. It's not always easy, but it's completely normal.
- There are outward physical changes that help us determine when the inward changes are due to occur: things like underarm hair, sweating, and sometimes acne or pimples. These are physical signs of maturity.

- You are not a man yet, but you have started the process. It is important as you travel this road that you have someone you can trust who will always speak honestly to you and will look out for your best interests. This needs to be someone who has walked that road and can give you the benefit of his experience. That is why I have brought you here—to talk to you about the things reserved for men to discuss.
- There are no questions that are off limits for this discussion.
- I will be completely honest with you.
- I will not hide anything from you that should be shared with a young man of your years.
- I will answer all your questions to the best of my ability.
- What we discuss here is a conversation between men and it must stay between us. You are not to discuss these things with any younger brothers. They are not ready for such discussions, and when they are I will discuss these things with them just as I am discussing them with you. Obviously, these discussions aren't for girls to hear, either, even though we will spend some time talking about girls.
- Many of the things you have heard and seen about girls and about being a man—things you think may be true and accurate—probably aren't. I want to tell you the truth about becoming a man, and what being a real man is all about.
- Preach the gospel to your son

□ 6. Male and Female Anatomy

- Under-arm hair and facial hair
- Body odor
- Growth spurts
- Muscle development
- Pubic hair
- Circumcision
- Erections

- Orgasms
- Wet dreams
- Masturbation
- A True Man: Physical vs. Character Traits (humility, courage; purity, faithfulness, selflessness, and self-control)

☐ 7. How to Treat Women

- Created in God's image
- Equal but different
- Strength as a blessing
- Thought life
- Self-control
- Speech
- Passion and purity

☐ 8. Sex

- Having Sex versus Making Love
- God's Plan for Sex (within marriage)
- How to "Do It"
- What is "Going Too Far?"
- What is Love (1Corinthians 13:4–8)
- Growing a Relationship Without Sex

☐ 9. Sexual Perversions

- What is perversion? Romans 1:8–13
- Lost but not without hope
- A few types of perversion: Pornography, Lust, Premarital sex, Adultery, Orgies, Homosexuality, Bisexuality, Pedophelia
- Perversion is sin, the same as yours and mine
- How to love and correct a person caught in a perverted lifestyle

☐ 10. What Is Safe Sex?

☐ *Sexually Transmitted Diseases*

- Two types of Sexually Transmitted Diseases: bacterial and viral
- Bacterial STDs include Chlamydia, syphilis, gonorrhea, and others. If treated properly with antibiotics, they can usually be cured.
- Viral STDs include HIV/AIDS, genital warts, some forms of herpes, and others. Viral STDs cannot be cured.
- In 2009 there were more than thirty known STDs, 15 percent of which are viral infections and therefore incurable.
- There is no such thing as safe sex outside of God's protective plan.

☐ *Birth Control*

- God tells us to avoid premarital sex for our good and his glory.
- Only sex within God's plan can ever be complete and truly fulfilling.
- Should you require birth control there are a variety of forms to choose from.
- To choose to have premarital sex is to step outside of God's plan for you, your wife, and your family.

☐ 11. Abuse and Abusers

- Substance
- Physical
- Verbal

☐ 12. Work and Career

- Giftings and interests
- Work as a joy

- Excellence in work
- Competition starts now
- Riches and virtues

☐ 13. Considering a Wife

- He who finds a wife finds a good thing
- Salvation
- Past history
- Medications
- Mental Illness

☐ Ending the Talk

- Let your son know that you are always available.
- You will continue to discuss these things with him as he continues to mature.
- Pray with your son for his wisdom, his work, his wife, his family, his obedience to God in all these things.

Forms of Birth Control

Outlined below are the most common forms of birth control, divided into categories for ease of comprehension. Each method includes a brief explanation of how it is intended to work. Non-abstinence birth control methods offer no real protection from STDs, and protect from pregnancy only to varying degrees.

It is not my intention that you necessarily walk through each of these methods with your son. This information is provided so you can become generally knowledgeable about these methods in order to address any questions that may arise, referring to this information if necessary during The Talk.

BEHAVIORAL METHODS

Method	Description	Effectiveness
Abstinence	The decision to abstain from all sexual relations prior to marriage.	The only 100% effective means of preventing pregnancy and avoiding STDs. No negative side effects.
Natural Family Planning	A variety of methods involving periodic abstinence from sex. Each method is designed to help a couple know on which days of the woman's cycle she is most likely to get pregnant, so they can avoid intercourse on those days.	If carefully and consistently observed, can be up to 90% effective in preventing pregnancy. No protection against STDs.

SURGICAL, CHEMICAL, AND DEVICE METHODS

Method	Description	Effectiveness
Sterilization	Tubal sterilization (also known as "tying the tubes") involves closing both of a woman's fallopian tubes (the tubes in which the egg is fertilized by the sperm) by tying or otherwise sealing them so that the eggs and sperm cannot come together. Men can be sterilized by the surgical procedure known as a vasectomy where the vas deferens (the tube that carries sperm from the testicles) is clamped, cut, or otherwise sealed to prevent sperm from being released during ejaculation.	Essentially 100% effective in preventing pregnancy, and irreversible. No protection against STDs.
Diaphragm	A soft rubber, latex, or silicone cup that is inserted into a woman's vagina prior to sexual intercourse, covering her cervix. It is designed to stop sperm from entering the cervical canal. It can also hold a spermicidal jelly or cream intended to kill sperm that manage to swim around the rim of the diaphragm.	No better than 94% effective in preventing pregnancy, and much less if the diaphragm is not properly inserted. No protection against STDs.

Method	Description	Effectiveness
Male Condom	A tube-like sheath, closed at one end, that is fitted over the erect penis before penetration. When ejaculation occurs, the semen collects inside the condom, preventing sperm from fertilizing an egg.	No better than 97% effective in preventing pregnancy when used correctly. Substantial protection against some STDs when used correctly.
Female Condom	A lubricated plastic sheath that lines the entire vaginal area, from labia to cervix.	No better than 95% effective in preventing pregnancy when used correctly. Substantial protection against some STDs when used correctly.
Intrauterine Devices (IUD)	A device made of soft, flexible plastic in a T shape, the same shape as the uterus, placed in the uterus by a physician. There are two types of IUDs: Levonorgestrel (LNg) and Copper. Both produce an environment in the womb that kills sperm.	No better than 99% effective in preventing pregnancy when inserted and used correctly. No protection from STDs.
Spermicides	Chemical foams, creams, jellies, film, or suppositories inserted into the vagina up to 15 minutes before intercourse. Spermicides create a barrier that kills sperm on contact and inhibits their movement up the vagina and into the cervix, preventing fertilization of an egg.	No better than 94% effective in preventing pregnancy when used alone and properly. A condom can enhance the effectiveness of this contraceptive method. No protection against STDs.

HORMONAL METHODS

Each of these methods delivers synthetic hormones intended to prevent the release of eggs from the ovaries and thicken the cervical mucus, which helps block sperm from entering the uterus.

Method	Description	Effectiveness
Birth Control Pill	A tablet taken orally by a woman for 21 to 28 days, or continuously.	92% effective for birth control. No protection against STDs.

Birth Control Patch	A patch that delivers hormones to a woman transdermally (through the skin and into the bloodstream).	92 to 98% effective for birth control, depending on the user's weight. No protection against STDs.
Implants	Matchstick-size, hormone-containing capsules surgically implanted in a woman's upper arm.	No better than 99% effective in preventing pregnancy. No protection against STDs.
Injectables	Hormones are injected into the woman's body.	No better than 99% effective in preventing pregnancy when received on a timely and consistent basis. No protection against STDs.
Vaginal Ring	A soft, flexible ring, about two inches in diameter, inserted into the vagina, delivers low doses of hormones.	No better than 98% effective in preventing pregnancy when used correctly. No protection against STDs.

ABORTIVE METHODS

Abortion is a tragedy of huge proportions. It takes the life of an unborn child and frequently causes physical, psychological, and emotional trauma to the mother as well as psychological and emotional trauma to the father.

Method	Description	Effectiveness
Morning-After Pill	Emergency contraception (also known as the morning-after pill or abortion pill) is a high-dose birth control pill. When taken up to 72 hours after sexual intercourse, it can result in fertilized eggs being dislodged from the ovarian walls, thus aborting a pregnancy.	No ability to prevent pregnancy when used as intended. Close to 100% effective in aborting a pregnancy. There is no clarity yet on the long-term medical implications to the mother. No protection against STDs.
Abortion	The discontinuation of pregnancy in any manner specifically intended to prevent a live birth.	No ability to prevent pregnancy when used as intended. However, most forms of abortion are 100% effective in preventing a live birth by killing the living unborn child. No protection against STDs.

196

Facts about Substance Abuse

H ere are some basic facts about substance abuse to consider passing along to your son.

Alcohol

- Alcohol is the most commonly used drug among young people.[5]
- On average, boys first try alcohol at age eleven and girls at age thirteen.
- The average American begins drinking regularly at 15.9 years old.

- Alcohol kills 6.5 times more youth under the national drinking age of twenty-one than all other illegal drugs combined.[6]
- The three top causes of death for fifteen to twenty-four-year-olds are car crashes, homicides, and suicides. Alcohol is a leading factor in all three.
- Youth who drink are fifty times more likely to use cocaine than those who never drink.[7]
- Among those who start drinking at age fourteen or younger, 40 percent later develop alcohol dependence, compared with 10 percent of those who begin drinking at age twenty or older.[8]

Tobacco

- Most people who smoke began smoking as adolescents.
- Teens who smoke are three times more likely than nonsmokers to use alcohol, eight times more likely to use marijuana, and twenty-two times more likely to use cocaine.
- Tobacco, whether smoked, chewed, or snuffed, causes cancer.
- Smoking is associated with other risky behaviors, such as fighting and engaging in unprotected sex.

Prescription Medications

Prescription medications are widely abused by both young people and adults. Young people usually obtain them from medicine cabinets in the home. Commonly abused drugs include the following.

- Opioids such as Oxycodone (OxyContin), hydrocodone (Vicodin), and meperidine (Demerol).
- Central Nervous System (CNS) Depressants such as pentobarbital sodium (Nembutal), diazepam (Valium), and alprazolam (Xanax).
- Stimulants such as Methylphenidate (Ritalin), amphetamine/dextroamphetamine (Adderall), and atomoxetine (Strattera).

Over-the-Counter Medications

It is possible to abuse or get addicted to cough, cold, sleep, or diet medications, including dextromethorphan, Coricidin, and others.

Inhalants

This is the dangerous habit of getting high by inhaling the fumes of some common household products such as glue, gasoline, paint, solvents, or various aerosol products. Known by such street names as huffing, sniffing, and wanging, this practice is estimated to claim the lives of more than a thousand children each year.

Many other young people, including some first-time users, are left with serious respiratory problems and/or permanent brain damage.

Marijuana

The average marijuana user starts at age fourteen. Side effects of persistent marijuana use include changes in the brain that affect your response to stress, motivation, and reward. Heavy users may have difficulty having children when they get older. Marijuana smoke has 50 to 70 percent more carcinogens (cancer-causing substances) than cigarette smoke. As with smoking of any kind, respiratory problems are more likely, including increased mucus, chronic cough, and bronchitis.

Stimulants and Psychedelics

Besides various prescription and over-the-counter medications, stimulants include cocaine and methamphetamines. The possible long-term effects of most stimulants include dependence, violence and aggression, and malnutrition due to suppression of appetite. In 1997, an estimated 1.5 million Americans age twelve and older were chronic cocaine users. Crack, a powerfully addictive stimulant, is the term for a smokeable form of cocaine.

"Club drugs" are stimulants or psychedelics used by teens and young adults at all-night dance parties, sometimes called "raves" or "trances." MDMA (Ecstasy), GHB, Rohypnol (Rophies), ketamine, methamphetamine, and LSD (a psychedelic) are some of the club or party drugs gaining popularity. Ten percent of teens say they have been to a rave, with Ecstasy reportedly available at more than two thirds of these raves. Twenty-eight percent of teens know a friend or classmate who has used Ecstasy, with 17 percent knowing more than one user.[9]

Because some club drugs are colorless, tasteless, and odorless, they can be added unobtrusively to beverages by individuals who want to intoxicate or sedate others. In recent years, there has been an increase in reports of club drugs being used to facilitate sexual assaults.

Depressants

Besides various prescription and over-the-counter medications, depressants include heroin, morphine, opium, and others. Used medicinally to relieve anxiety, irritability, and tension, depressants have a high potential for abuse. When combined with alcohol, the intoxicating effects are heightened and the risks are multiplied. New, young drug users are being lured by inexpensive, high-purity heroin that can be sniffed or smoked instead of injected. Once primarily an inner-city drug, heroin is now increasingly common in affluent communities.

Steroids

Anabolic steroids are a group of powerful compounds closely related to the male hormone testosterone. As more and more professional and Olympic athletes are exposed as steroid users, these drugs are increasingly used by athletes at the college level and below. There have been recent significant increases in anabolic steroid abuse even among middle-schoolers.

Steroids are typically abused not to change how you feel, but how you look and perform on the sports field. Steroid abuse is about creating a false reputation for yourself. Prolonged use can cause significant physical and mental problems.

Notes

1. Jacqui Bailey, *Sex, Puberty and All That Stuff: A Guide to Growing Up* (Hauppauge, New York: Baron's Educational Series, Inc., 2004), 51.

2. Ruth Bell, *Changing Bodies, Changing Lives*, 3rd ed. (New York: Three Rivers Press, 1998), 106.

3. Bailey, *Sex Puberty and All That Stuff*, 69.

4. Lynda Madaras, *The 'What's Happening to My Body?' Book for Boys: A Growing-Up Guide for Preteens and Teens* (New York: Newmarket Press, 1983), 149.

5. Michael Gurian, *A Fine Young Man: What Parents, Mentors and Educators Can Do to Shape Adolescent Boys into Exceptional Men* (New York, Penguin Putnam, Inc., 1999), 139.

6. Dinal Craik, "Friendship" in *The Best Loved Poems of the American People* (New York: Doubleday, 1936).

7. If communicating with your son has proven difficult or impossible in the past, consider reading Rick Horne's book *Get Outta My Face: How to Reach Angry, Unmotivated Teens with Biblical Counsel*. Rick does a masterful job of teaching us how to effectively communicate with our teens even if they tend to be abrasive or unreceptive.

8. Centers for Disease Control

9. For more information on teens and STDs, consider Pam Stenzel's DVD "Sex Has a Price Tag." Pam's dynamic presentation of the facts and risks of teen sex meets teens right at their level with powerful and life-changing information www.pamstenzel.com. For the most up-to-date STD statistics visit the STD section of the Centers for Disease Control website (www.cdc.gov/std).

10. Partnership For A Drug-Free America
11. Substance Abuse: The Nation's Number One Health Problem
12. Substance Abuse: The Nation's Number One Health Problem
13. National Survey of Substance Abuse Attitudes, Feb. 2001
14. Mothers Against Drunk Driving
15. National Survey of Substance Abuse Attitudes, Feb. 2001